D0283745

Complete Speaker's Galaxy of Funny Stories, Jokes and Anecdotes

Winston K. Pendleton

Parker Publishing Company, Inc.

West Nyack, New York

Acknowledgment is gratefully given for quotations from *2121 Funny Stories and How to Tell Them*, and *505 Jokes You Can Tell*, Copyright © Bethany Press, St. Louis Mo.

10 9 8 7

Library of Congress Cataloging in Publication Data

Pendleton, Winston K
Complete speaker's galaxy of funny stories, jokes, and anecdotes.

Includes index.
1. Public speaking--Handbooks, manuals, etc.
2. American wit and humor. II. Title.
PN4193.I5P4 817'.5'408 79-10027

Printed in the United States of America

For darling Gladys,
with many thanks and much gratitude
for always laughing at me—even at times
when I wasn't funny.

How This *Galaxy* Will Help Your Speech

Humor is very often the magical ingredient that can transform your speech into a power-packed address that ends with the audience on its feet applauding. The same secret applies to conversation. When you tell the right story at the right time, the peals of laughter that follow will let you know that your conversation is right on target.

The important question, though, is where to find the appropriate story or anecdote that will add just the right touch of humor to your next speech or put the extra sparkle into your conversation.

Complete Speaker's Galaxy of Funny Stories, Jokes and Anecdotes is the answer to that question. This invaluable speaker's guide is a gold mine of audience-tested, laugh-getting material that will provoke spontaneous reaction to your next speech.

While this book will undoubtedly amuse you with its 829 funny entries, this is not its function. Instead, it provides the raw material you can use to make other people laugh.

This resource book has been written and organized with you, the speaker, in mind. As a speaker myself, I know how important it is to be able to find quickly all the stories and jokes that are just right for your speech. This *Complete Speaker's Galaxy* features three separate and distinct keys for finding exactly what you need at a moment's notice.

The Table of Contents immediately directs you to each of the 365 major categories, which are arranged in alphabetical order throughout the book. Once you have read and evaluated the material under the heading you've selected, you'll find right there, at your fingertips, the numbers of related stories located elsewhere in this galaxy. So you can flip immediately to this additional material, giving you an even larger selection to consider.

The third valuable key for pinpointing appropriate humorous material is the Thematic Index. This bonus feature gives you 605 additional themes for locating the joke, story or anecdote that's just perfect for your use.

When you add humor to a speech, you are like a master chef who adds spices and seasoning to the various dishes on the menu. He might put a pinch of salt in the soup, a few coriander seeds in the salad or two or three sprigs of rosemary with the roast. If done properly, a mess of tasteless pottage becomes a gourmet's delight.

So it is with humor. Sprinkle it skillfully in the proper parts of your speech and the results will be just as masterful.

For example, open your speech with a funny joke or anecdote to attract attention. Then, tell a funny personal experience to build rapport with your listeners and help them relax. As you listen to their laughter, you will discover that they are helping you to relax at the same time. During the body of your speech, use humor to make a point and to keep your audience alert and hold their attention. Finally, with the *right* funny story, you can bring your speech to a dramatic ending that combines laughter with applause.

But what is that *right* story? What makes people laugh?

Above all else, if you want to make people laugh, they must be able to picture what you are talking about. You must meet with them on familiar ground. Your funny story must fit a time and place that they can relate to.

You must have the right material.

For example, if you were speaking to a convention of Jaycees, you must remember that not one of them had been born when Hitler marched into Poland. They never heard of Roosevelt meeting at Potsdam with Stalin except in their history books. They were not even in elementary school when Harry Truman became President. And their only knowledge of the "great depression" comes from what their parents and grandparents tell them. Try telling a Calvin Coolidge joke to that crowd and see how much laughter you generate.

For this reason, the stories, jokes and anecdotes in this book are *timeless*. They were selected for that reason. You are supposed to give them a present day perspective. Make them live. Modernize them. Keep them up to date.

If you think that adding a name to a story will make it better, go ahead and do it. But use somebody who is in today's news and not in the history books. Even when you put a movie star's name in a story, you had better be careful—their popularity fades quickly.

Keep this in mind. Today's audiences are sophisticated. They have heard the best professional comedians on television. That is why you must use timeless material that can be changed and updated and made to sound new and fresh when you tell it.

Remember, too, as you begin to fit humorous stories into your speech, that the biggest laughs come when you make yourself the butt of the joke. Tell stories about your own hometown, your street, your kids, your dog, your golf game, your shortcomings.

With these principles in mind, the *Complete Speaker's Galaxy of Funny Stories, Jokes and Anecdotes* stands ready to make your next speech sparkle with wit and humor.

Just follow the easy directions outlined below:

HOW TO USE THIS BOOK

A Working Example

First, let's set the scene. Suppose you are invited to give the kickoff speech at the United Givers luncheon. You will be speaking to the teams, men and women, who will do the work. You want to inspire them to do a super job—their very best. You are the main speaker and you have been given the closing twenty minutes on the program. Of course, you want to do a super job yourself. So, you plan to add some zip and zest to your talk with a few funny stories.

Before you open the book, decide how many stories you will need. If you have only twenty minutes on the program, and if you have anything important to say, four or five stories will be enough. A story often fills as much as two minutes—or even a bit more—counting the laughter that follows. With that in mind, you can figure that four or five stories will take six to eight minutes of your time.

Now start looking. Remembering that people love stories that reflect on you, turn to the category "Speaker." There you will find twelve laugh getters plus a cross reference at the end of the category that leads you to six other related stories. Select a couple and reword them so that they fit you. You might do it this way, "The other day I was speaking to (name an actual group) in (name a real place) and . . . ." When you introduce the story that way, you are bound to get a good response.

Once you have your opening stories in mind, you can begin searching for a story or two that might illustrate one of your main points. Let us say you are going to emphasize the importance of "Attitude." You can find that under a main heading with another reference listed below it. What about telling about the power of "Enthusiasm"? That, too, is a main category with a cross reference. So is "Persuasion" (which they must use to get a contribution from a stubborn or stingy contributor). And that's another word to look up, "Contribution." (Incidentally, story 175 under "Contribution," about the Star Spangled Banner, would be a great one to use as a closer. It's about a United Givers luncheon speaker.) When you urge the team members to put forth their best "Effort" and be "Persistent," you can find those subjects listed in the Index.

And that's the way it goes. In fifteen or twenty minutes you have found more stories than you can use in a twenty minute speech.

The material is here. Enough to last a speaker a lifetime. Every story in this book has "brought down the house" at one time or another. So, happy hunting as you search out the *right* story for your next speech.

And best wishes for lots of laughs.

Winston K. Pendleton

CONTENTS

LOOK HERE FIRST

These 365 categories make it easy to find a story to fit your speech.

HERE IS YOUR GALAXY OF STORIES

You Can Use It Three Ways to Find the Exact Story You Need

* * *

FIRST: Look for it under its broad subject. You have 365 categories to choose from, listed alphabetically.

SECOND: Refer to the numbers that you will find at the end of some of the listings. They will lead you to other related stories.

THIRD: Look in the Thematic Index at the back of the book for still other related listings.

ACCIDENT

1. A man from a small town was visiting the city. After asking directions from several persons with negative results, he spotted a policeman directing traffic at an intersection. Watching traffic carefully, he finally dashed between the passing cars to where the policeman stood.

Almost out of breath he said, "Can you please tell me how to get to City Memorial Hospital?"

"That's easy," the policeman said. "You stand right where you are for about five minutes and an ambulance will be along to take you there."

2. A youngster rushed into the country store and shouted, "My Dad was fixing the roof and the ladder slipped out from under him and he is hanging from the eaves."

The manager of the store said, "Okay, son, we'll rescue him." Then he yelled at all the fellows sitting around the store, "Hey, let's go. On the double, everybody, before he gets too tired and has to turn loose."

But before they could move, the youngster said, "Before you run too fast, will you please help me put some film in my camera?"

3. When the man answered the phone, the voice on the other end said, "Mr. Jones, this is Les Henderson's garage. Your wife just drove into the garage a few minutes ago to have a new air conditioner hose installed and I was calling to ask if you are going to pay for . . . ."

"Yes," Jones said, interrupting the caller, "I'll pay for the hose. Just send me the bill."

"Oh," the voice said, "I'm not calling about the air conditioner hose. Your wife already paid for that. I want to know if you intend to pay for the side of my garage that she knocked out when she drove in?"

4. A patrolman arrived at the scene of an accident to find a woman lying unconscious a few feet from an automobile. A small crowd had gathered, and a man was trying feverishly to revive the woman.

"Who was driving this car?" the patrolman asked.

"I was," said the man who was helping the woman.

"How did you hit her?" the patrolman asked.

"Oh, I didn't hit her," the man said. "As I approached the intersection I saw that she was trying to cross the street. So, I stopped for her and she fainted."

5. Supper was over. The father of the house and his nine-year-old son were in the living room watching television. Mother and daughter were in the kitchen washing up the supper dishes.

Suddenly father and son heard a terrible crashing sound of something being broken in the kitchen. They waited for a moment in shock but didn't hear a sound.

"It was Mom who broke the dish," the boy said.

"How do you know?" his father asked.

"Because," his son said, "she isn't saying anything."

6. A man's wife had scratched the side of their new car as she backed it out of the garage.

"Don't worry about it," her husband said. "Those things happen. Take it to the body repair shop and have it touched up."

As fate would have it, two weeks later she backed into a light pole and broke the right rear tail light. She was almost in tears when she told her husband about it.

"It's just bad luck," he said. "Don't worry about it. Take it to the body repair shop and have it fixed."

"But," she said, "I'm so embarrassed to take it back there again."

"If you are embarrassed," he said, "just tell them that I did it."

"That's what is so embarrassing," she said. "I told them that the last time."

7. The judge was trying a case against an insurance company. A man who had been walking along a country road was struck and injured by an automobile. The attorney for the insurance company was trying to convince the jury that the driver of the car was not at fault. He said, "The plaintiff was obviously in the wrong. The driver of the car is a careful driver. He has been driving a car for more than 25 years and has never had an accident. I think that tells the story. And, on that, we rest our case."

"Wonderful," shouted the lawyer for the plaintiff. "If you are basing this case on experience, I would remind you that my client has been walking for 60 years."

8. "My goodness," a fellow said to his friend, "what happened to your face? I never saw such a mess."

"Well," his friend said, "you have been hearing all this stuff about how you should talk to your plants. I decided to try it. Yesterday I had a long and intimate conversation with that honeysuckle vine that is growing up the oak tree in my back yard. When we were saying goodbye to each other and I was telling it I would see it again today, it said to me, 'Oh, by the way. I'm not a honeysuckle. I'm a poison ivy.' "

9. From the kitchen came the sound of the crash of either broken glass or broken china.

"Willy," cried his mother from the living room, "what on earth are you doing in the kitchen?"

"Nothing," Willy said, "it's already done."

10. A man was injured in an accident aboard a bus, and his friends told him that he should sue for damages.

"I don't want any damages," he said. "I've been damaged enough. What I want is repairs."

11. A crew was unloading a tank car of highly explosive chemicals when it exploded. Two men were killed and half a dozen were knocked unconscious. As the ambulance attendants were carrying one of the men on a stretcher he regained consciousness. Just as he did, his hand fell over the side of the stretcher. Feeling nothing but air, he let out a great moan and said, "Oh, my, God. I haven't even hit ground yet."

214, 226, 548.

ACCURACY

12. The sales manager had hired a new secretary and was describing her duties. "One of your duties will be to double check the expense accounts that the salesmen send in. They are notorious when it comes to arithmetic. So, to be sure you have it exactly right, I want you to add those figures three times before you bring them in for me to approve."

The next morning the new secretary entered his office with a cheerful smile. "Here is the first expense account," she said. "I did what you told me. I added the figures three times. And here are the three totals."

754.

ACTOR

13. Two friends were talking about an actor friend of theirs who had been sick. "He went to two or three specialists and none of them could help him," the first friend said. "Then his wife figured out his problem and cured him in three days."

"What did she do?" the other man asked.

"She fed him massive doses of sugar," the first fellow said. "Didn't you ever hear of a sugar-cured ham?"

14. A Hollywood actor had been called into court as a witness in an accident case. When he was asked to identify himself he gave his name and said, "I am probably one of the world's greatest actors."

On the way home from the trial, his wife said to him, "Why in the world did you have to brag like that? It would have been much more becoming if you had been more modest."

"I understand what you mean," he said, "and ordinarily I wouldn't have said such a thing. But in this case I was under oath."

15. A hopeless young actor had been given a part in a Broadway play because he was a nephew of the man who was backing the show financially. He was given a simple part with only one line to say. In scene three someone was supposed to rush on stage and shoot him. His one line was, "My God, I am shot."

In spite of all the coaching he could give the young fellow, the director couldn't teach him to say the line properly.

"Say it right," the director would say. "My God, I am *shot*."

And the young fellow would either speak his words in an unexcited monotone or with the wrong emphasis, such as, "My God, *I* am shot."

Finally, in desperation the director figured out a trick. On opening night he would put rubber bullets in the gun so that the man would be shot, but not hard enough to hurt him. He figured that in his surprise the young man might speak naturally—and of course say his lines correctly.

Came the big night. The big scene. The shot. And the actor said, "My God, I *am* shot."

ADVENTURE

16. The big game hunter was telling about his adventures to a group of school children during their show-and-tell period. In describing some of his exciting experiences in Africa he said, "One night I remember being wakened by a great roaring noise. I jumped up and grabbed my gun, which I always kept loaded at the foot of my cot. I rushed out and killed a huge lion in my pajamas."

At the close of his presentation he asked if there were any questions.

"Yes," said a little girl sitting on the front row, "how did the lion get into your pajamas?"

ADVICE

17. A businessman was giving his son some advice as he was preparing to go away to college. "I think it fine that you are going to study business administration. I would suggest one thing. Be sure to take at least one course in business law."

"Why is that?" his son asked. "I'm going into business, not law."

"Well," his father said. "In business, honesty always is the best policy. Above all, you must be honest. And if you take a course in business law, you will learn about all sorts of clever things you can do—and still be honest."

18. A young woman who had been married only three weeks called the newspaper and asked for the food editor.

"Would you please help me?" she said. "My husband's mother and father are coming to a special dinner tomorrow night. It's in honor of my husband's boss and his wife. I've never cooked a big dinner before and I want everything to be perfect. So, I bought a nine pound frozen turkey at the supermarket. I am going to cook it in our new micro-wave oven. I wonder if you could tell me how long I should cook it?"

"Just a minute," the food editor said as he turned to check in his big reference cook book. He put the phone down so quickly that he didn't hear the young bride say, "Oh, thank you so much. You've been such a big help," before she hung up.

379, 464, 594.

AGE

19. The tourist with a camera around his neck had stopped beside a tumble-down shack on a mountain road. Sitting on the porch in a rocking chair was the perfect picture of a rugged old mountaineer.

"May I take your picture?" the tourist asked.

"All right with me," the man said. "Go ahead."

After he had made two or three exposures, the tourist said, "I've always wondered how you mountain people live to such a ripe old age. What is your secret?"

"No secret how I live," he said. "Everybody around here knows. I drink a quart of home-made whiskey every day, smoke half a dozen cigars that I make myself from my own home-grown tobacco and I chase after all the neighborhood gals."

"That seems like a rather strenuous life for a man of your age," the tourist said. "Just how old are you anyway?"

"I'll be 32, come October," the man said.

20. Several women were chatting at a bridge party. One, who was suspected of being much older than she claimed, said with a sad face, "My, I hate to think of life at 40."

One of her friends couldn't miss the opportunity to say, "What happened to you then?"

21. The neighborhood was celebrating the 100th birthday of their beloved eldest citizen. Among other exciting events, he was being interviewed on television. "You look pretty healthy," the young reporter said, "Are you able to get around and walk very much these days?"

"Why certainly," the old man said with a grin, "I can walk a lot better today than I could a hundred years ago."

22. Two housewives who were close friends decided they would go back to work now that their children were grown. They went together to apply for employment at a large manufacturing plant.

They were sitting side by side as they filled in the long and detailed application form. As one of the women came to the little box marked "age" she sat staring out of the window as though in deep thought.

Her friend leaned over and whispered, "Go ahead and put it down. The longer you wait, the worse it gets."

23. Members of the family were helping grandfather celebrate his eightieth birthday. One of his granddaughters said to him, "You look so happy today. Doesn't it bother you to grow old?"

"Bother me?" he said. "Heck no, it doesn't bother me. I enjoy it. I look forward to getting older and older and older. Because the very moment when I quit getting older, I'm dead."

24. A wife said to her husband, "I don't think I look 35, do you?"

"No I don't," he said, "but you used to."

87, 336, 455, 457, 534, 628.

AILMENT

25. The woman was helping her bent-over husband to a seat in the doctor's office. The doctor's receptionist asked the woman in a sympathetic tone, "And what is his problem? Arthritis with complications?"

"No," the man's wife said, "do-it-yourself with a wheelbarrow full of bricks."

AIRLINE

26. A woman was arguing with the airline ticket agent who had told her that the plane from Chicago was going to be late.

"I don't understand how anything that flies at 680 miles an hour can be late," she said.

27. A woman was on her first airplane ride and was seated next to the window over the wing. As the plane took off through a heavy mist and climbed toward its cruising altitude, the pilot kept his cruising lights on. For half an hour the woman watched the light blinking on the end of the wing, then she rang the bell for the stewardess. When she came, the woman said to her, "Excuse me, Miss, but would you tell the pilot that he forgot to turn off his right turn indicator?"

28. "This is a great airline," the man said. "We had our breakfast in New York, our lunch in Chicago, our dinner in San Francisco, and our baggage in Dallas."

719, 772.

AIRPLANE

29. The youngsters were trying to talk their grandmother into taking her first airplane ride.

"Not me," she said. "I don't go for all those new fangled things. I'm going to sit right here and enjoy television like the Lord intended."

374, 526.

ALARM CLOCK

30. Two women were chatting. "I have trouble getting my 13 year old boy up in the morning. Sometimes it's almost impossible to wake him up."

"Oh," her friend said. "I solved that a long time ago with my boy. When it's time to wake him up, I just toss the cat on his bed."

"How does that wake him up?" the first woman asked.

"Because," her friend said, "he sleeps with his dog."

ALLERGY

31. A certain housewife was allergic to mink coats. She got sick every time she saw one—on another woman.

108.

ANSWER

32. One young lady had the perfect answer when an eager old man tried to get familiar with her with the oldest approach in the book.

"Where have you been all my life?" he said.

"Well," she said, "for the first 45 years, I wasn't even born."

33. Certainly, men and women are different. At the supper table, if you ask a man, "Where did you get this cake?" he'll tell you "at the supermarket." Ask his wife and she'll say, "What's the matter with it?" Or, ask a woman how she bruised her toe and she'll say, "I kicked a chair." Ask her husband the same question and he'll say, "Somebody left a chair in the middle of the room."

593, 603.

APARTMENT

34. In spite of much protest from all four parents, two teenagers insisted on getting married. Finally, the parents consented and the marriage took place. The bride was "sweet 16" and the groom was 17.

After the honeymoon was over and they had returned home, they began to look for an apartment. After studying the classified advertisements in Sunday's newspaper all afternoon the bride moaned in despair, "It's awful. We can't find a place to live. It's unfair. All the apartments are for adults only."

561.

APPEARANCE

35. A doctor was talking to a woman about the condition of her husband, who was in the hospital for a checkup. "I don't like the looks of your husband," he said.

"I don't either," the woman said, "but I could have done worse. He has a good job and is nice to the children."

628.

APPRECIATION

36. The play looked like a sure success because after each scene the applause went on and on, most of it coming from the rear of the theater. As the play drew to a close, the audience called for encore after encore—again most of the applause came from the rear of the auditorium.

In the midst of the ovation, one usher who was applauding with great vigor said to another usher who was doing the same, "Great. Great. Keep it up. In just one more minute we'll be on overtime."

37. Following a hotly contested race for town councilmen in a small Southern town, this notice appeared in the weekly paper:

> "I wish to thank the 100 persons who signed my petition so that my name would appear on the ballot as a candidate for Town Councilman. I want to thank the 485 persons who promised to vote for me and the 340 who said they did. But, more than any of the others, I want to thank the 47 who did vote for me. George Brown."

61, 753.

ARCHITECT

38. A rich businessman retired and moved to Florida. He brought with him a set of plans for his "retirement dream home" that had been drawn up by a noted architect. Wishing to get away from the rush-rush-rush of city life, he bought ten acres of wooded land in a small village well off the beaten path and sought the help of a local builder.

"I already have the plans for the house," the businessman told the builder, "and I'd like you to follow them exactly. Can you do that?"

"Sure, I can follow plans," the man said. "Let me look at them." After checking the plans over carefully, the man said, "Why, these plans are ridiculous. They are stupid. You can't build a house like this."

"What do you mean?" the businessman said. "Those plans were drawn up by one of the best architects in the United States. And that's the way I want the house built."

"Well, it's your house," the builder said. "And I'll build it this crazy way if you want. But, if you follow these stupid plans you're going to end up with four bathrooms in your house."

ARGUMENT

39. Two men were chatting over a pitcher of beer in a bar.

"Well, here we are again," the first man said to his friend, "seeking refuge from a miserable home life. I suppose you had a fight last night again with your wife?"

"Yes, I did," said his friend.

"How did it end?" the first man asked.

"In the end my wife came to me on her hands and knees," his friend said.

"She did?" the first man said with wonderment. "What did she say?"

"She said 'come out from under that bed, you skunk, and fight like a man!' "

40. A husband and wife were having a heated argument. At the height of their dispute the wife screamed, "I wish I had never married you. I should have taken my mother's advice."

"Do you mean to tell me," her husband said, "that your mother urged you not to marry me?"

"Yes, that's exactly what I'm saying. She told me a thousand times to have nothing to do with you."

"Gosh," he said, "and to think how I have misjudged that poor woman all these years."

ARITHMETIC

41. The husband was tired of spending hours each month trying to balance his wife's bank statement. They finally agreed on a plan. She would sort out the checks and try her best to make the statement come out the same as her stubs. If it balanced, fine. If it didn't, then her husband would help.

Once, after working on her accounts all evening, she finally said to him, "This time I've made it balance. Do you want to check it out?"

Sure enough, the balance from the bank checked with the balance in her check book. But, just to be sure, the husband checked over some of her figures, "Washing machine payment, $38.50, lights $62.38, department store $47.80." The final entry read, "ESP $1.66."

"This looks great," he said, "but what in the world is ESP $1.66?"

"Oh," she said, "that means 'Error Some Place.' "

42. The teacher was trying to teach simple subtraction. "Now, Hugh," she said, "if your father earned $180 a week and if they deducted $6.00 for insurance, $10.80 for Social Security, and $24.00 for taxes, and then if he gave your mother half, what would she have?"

"A heart attack," the kid said.

43. A boy was doing his homework and said to his father, "Dad, can you help me with this problem? If a man earns $200 a week and his wife spends $210 for . . ."

"Stop right there, son," the boy's father said. "You'll have to ask your mother to help you with that. She's a specialist in that kind of arithmetic."

75, 337.

ARMY

44. This was the Second Lieutenant's first command. As he lined his platoon up for his initial inspection, he said to them, "I hope we'll have a good relationship together. I want you to respect me as your leader. At the same time, I want you to know that if you have any problems you can feel free to talk to me about them just as though I were your father."

One fresh recruit took the Lieutenant at his word and called out, "Hey, Dad, how about borrowing your jeep for a date tonight?"

ARREST

45. The patrolman had stopped a woman who was speeding. He asked to see her driver's license and said, "Lady, you were going 50 miles an hour in a 35 mile an hour zone."

As she handed him her license, she said, "Before you begin writing that ticket, I think we should get our priorities straight. Are you supposed to advise me of my constitutional rights first, or am I supposed to tell you that my son is head of the highway patrol?"

ART

46. Three men broke into the Greenwich Village studio of a famous modernistic painter. They tied up the artist, forced open his wall safe and fled with $46,000 in cash. The next day the artist was found by friends and released. He immediately called the police.

"Would you be able to identify the robbers?" the detective said.

"Oh, certainly," the artist said. "That's my business, remembering what things look like. I'll draw you a picture of them."

He drew the picture and gave it to the police. The next day they arrested the Brooklyn Bridge, a one-eyed go-go dancer and a garbage truck.

47. Some housewives were attending their weekly art class. The instructor was talking about realism in art, and one of the women said, "I once heard about an artist who painted a cobweb so true to life that the cleaning woman spent 15 minutes trying to sweep it away."

"I don't believe it," said another woman.

"Why not?" asked the instructor. "Artists have been known to do such things."

"Artists, maybe," said the woman, "but never cleaning women."

48. A rather outspoken and opinionated photographer was attending a one-man art show. Being a friend of the artist, he felt he had a right to speak his mind. "You modern artists are a bunch of fakes," he said. "You just smear a lot of paint on the canvas and call it anything you want. This one, for example, would be a fried egg or a sunset—who can tell? I don't even pretend to like it. I believe in realism. When I look at a picture of something I want to see it exactly as it is. That's why I took up photography."

"Have you taken any good pictures lately?" the artist asked.

"Yes," the photographer said as he reached in his wallet. "Here's one I just took of my five year old granddaughter."

The artist studied the photograph very seriously for half a minute and then said, "Amazing. Is she really that tiny?"

630.

ATHLETICS

49. The class was taking its final examination on Ancient History. The question was, "Name two ancient sports "

The answer on one paper, "Antony and Cleopatra."

ATTENTION

50. "George," the man's wife said at the breakfast table one morning, "you will notice that I mended that hole in your pocket last night after you went to bed. Don't you think I'm a thoughtful and considerate wife?"

"I sure do," her husband said, "and I appreciate it. But tell me one thing. How did you discover that I had a hole in my pocket?"

231, 815.

ATTITUDE

51. "Always accentuate the positive," shouted the speaker. "Eliminate the negative. Use the word *is* instead of the word *not*."

One woman who attended his lecture said to her friend, "He's right. I'm going to quit making negative statements. I'm going to speak positively from now on."

"Like what?" her friend asked.

"Like I used to say that my husband was *not* fit to live with the hogs. Now I am going to say he *is* fit to live with them."

469.

AUTHOR

52. An author had written six novels, the last three having been on the best seller lists. Of course, he was appearing on TV shows and radio and was being invited to all sorts of parties and lionized in general. All of this attention had finally begun to go to his head, and he had developed the habit of constantly talking about himself and his books. One day, in a most kind and gentle manner, his wife pointed out his problem and suggested that he let other people talk about themselves more. He was smart enough to realize what had happened; so they worked out a signal. When his wife saw that he was talking too much about himself, she would cough and he would change the subject.

That evening, they were invited to a party and, sure enough, the author began to talk about himself. His wife coughed according to their plan, and the author said to the lady he was talking to, "Well, enough about me. Let's talk about you for awhile. What do you think of my latest book?"

53. A literary agent called one of his clients on the phone and said, "I have some good news and some bad news."

"Tell me the good news first," the writer said.

"Paramount loved that movie script you wrote; absolutely ate it up. Relished every word of it," he said.

"So, that's great," the writer said. "What's the bad news?"

"Paramount," the agent said, "is my collie dog."

54. The budding young poet was trying to persuade the publisher to publish his book of poetry.

"But you have never had any of your poems published," the publisher said, "not even in magazines."

"I know," the young man said, "but I've shown my poems to a lot of people, and they like what I've written. Let me read a letter I received last week. 'You are undoubtedly one of the most promising young poets in America today. You have the understanding of life of Tennyson, the simplicity of Longfellow, the verve of Lord Byron and the romantic zest of Shelley. More than that, I think you are one of the most sensitive and gracious young men in the world.' "

"My, that's some testimony to your work," the publisher said. "Who wrote the letter?"

"My mother," the young poet said.

55. A woman's manuscript had been returned from the publisher with the usual rejection slip. She was so irate that she called the publisher on the phone. "You publishers are all alike. You didn't even read my manuscript. You promised to read it if I sent it to you, but you didn't read it. I know, because I pasted the edges of all the pages from 150 to 160 together. And they came back that way. You didn't treat me right. How can you make a judgment without reading the manuscript?"

After some effort, the publisher managed to interrupt her to say, "Look, lady, a manuscript is like a soft boiled egg. When I open one at breakfast, I don't need to eat the whole egg to know that it's bad."

AUTOMOBILE

56. "Since I bought that new sports car," a fellow said to a friend, "I don't have to walk to the bank anymore to deposit my savings."

"That's right," his friend said, "now you drive don't you?"

"Not exactly," the first fellow said. "I don't go to the bank anymore because I don't have any savings to deposit."

57. A housewife was unable to get to the supermarket because she couldn't get her car started. After a half hour of frustration she finally called her husband at his office to ask what she should do.

"Did you try choking it?" he asked.

"No," she said, gritting her teeth, "but I sure felt like it."

751.

BABY

58. A woman was shopping in the toy department for a birthday present for her little girl.

The saleswoman had suggested a doll. "This is one of the loveliest dolls we have. Look. When you lay her down in her little crib she closes her eyes and goes right to sleep, just like a real live little girl."

"That's a pretty doll, all right," said the woman, "but from what you say I'm sure you have never had a real live little girl."

59. As a young mother was bathing her new baby, she remembered that she had used the last of the disposable diapers. "Oh my, you'll have to help me," she said to her six year old daughter. "Run down to the corner drug store and get a box of diapers."

To be sure the little girl didn't lose the money, Mamma put a five-dollar bill in an envelope and told her to be careful.

The little girl did as she was told, and when the clerk had wrapped the package, he said to her, "That will be $1.95 for the diapers and eight cents for the tax."

"Oh, we don't need any tacks," the little girl said. "I've watched Mamma change the baby, and she just ties the diapers on."

618.

BABYSITTER

60. The man and his wife returned home following a visit to the theater, and he said to the babysitter, "Well, I hope little Wendy was as good as gold while we were gone."

"She was for a while," the babysitter said, "but she went off the gold standard at about 9:30."

BANKER

61. The teller at the drive-in bank had pulled his shade down because the afternoon sun was hitting him directly in his eyes. He could see his customers as they drove up, but they couldn't see him. As one woman drove in, he punched the button and the money drawer rolled out just as she came to a stop. She dropped her check in the drawer rather gingerly, and it withdrew almost instantly. A moment later it rolled out again with her money in it. She picked up the money and looked around cautiously, but still couldn't see anybody. Then, looking at the drawer as it began to recede, she said, "I know you are completely automated, but I want to thank you anyway."

62. The bank had just installed a new burglar alarm. In case of a hold-up, all the teller had to do was to step on a pedal on the floor. This would ring a bell at police headquarters only three blocks away.

The first day it was in use, the bank was held up. The teller, before handing over the money, pressed his foot on the pedal. Immediately, the phone in the bank began to ring. As the teller reached for it, the hold-up man grabbed it himself and lifted the receiver.

"This is the Police Department," a voice said. "Did you know that somebody over there has stepped on the pedal that rings that new burglar alarm over here?"

63. A series of eight forged checks turned up in the bank within a two-week period. All of them had been cashed by the same teller. The bank president was talking to her about it and said, "Why didn't you check his identification more closely?"

"Because," she answered logically, "he looked so familiar."

64. A man was seated next to his banker at the regular weekly civic club luncheon. "Somebody told me you were looking for a cashier," the man said.

"Yes, we are," the banker said.

"But I thought you just hired one a month ago," the man said.

"We did," the banker said. "He's the one we are looking for."

65. The president of the bank had been losing his hair for a number of years and had become extremely sensitive about his growing bald spot. To ease his embarrassment, he always wore his hat in the office.

One day, a golfing buddy of his was visiting him in his office and the banker said, "We've been friends for a long time. Why is it you have never opened an account in my bank?"

"I have thought about it many times," the banker's friend said. "I even came in to open an account once. But I realized that if I had my money in your bank it would make me nervous since you always look as though you're ready to go someplace."

66. The man had been turned down by the bank for a loan. As he turned to leave the banker's office, he said, "I just talked to the wrong man. I really wanted to talk to the friendly free lending man whom I see every night in your television commercials."

67. A man was applying to the bank for an automobile loan. He said to the banker, "I notice that the sign on your desk says 'personal loan department.' What is a personal loan?"

"That's the kind of a loan we are making now," the banker explained. "When we make the loan we put it on the computer. We leave it there as long as you make you payments on time. But, if you ever miss a payment, that's when we get personal. And, incidentally, we can get very personal when you get behind."

68. A banker was chatting with a friend at their weekly civic club meeting. "When I was a little fellow," the banker said, "my ambition was to become a pirate."

"You must be very happy," his friend said, "few men in life ever realize their childhood dreams."

69. A banker was being interviewed about the business outlook.

"How do you feel about business trends during the next year?" the newspaperman asked.

"I'm optimistic," the banker said, "I think we're going to have the greatest business year this part of the country has ever seen. However, I am worried a bit about it."

"If you are so optimistic about the future," the newspaperman asked, "why are you worried?"

"I'm afraid," said the banker, "that my optimism might not be justified."

70. A man was reading the morning paper and said to his wife, "Hey, listen to this. The cashier at the bank has absconded with $60,000. Not only that, but he stole one of the bank's executive limousines and ran off with the bank president's wife."

"My, that's awful," said his wife. "I wonder who they will get to teach his Sunday school class next week?"

142, 273, 283, 387, 755.

BARBER

71. The day was hot and the child in the barber chair was wearing a little sun suit. Sensing that this was the first haircut the kid had ever had, the barber worked rapidly in spite of his little victim's screams and a mother who kept saying, "not too short, not too short."

The entire ordeal was over within six or seven minutes, and the child immediately ran to the mother, weeping and sobbing. "That's just about the worst haircut I ever saw," the woman said.

The barber was not too happy over the episode himself, and he said, "Look, lady, that's the same haircut I have been giving little boys for years."

"Boy!" cried the mother. "This is a girl!"

BARGAIN

72. A woman was shopping for a shawl for her grandmother. She found a beautiful hand knit woolen import, but was shocked to see that the price was $95.00.

"Are you sure the price is correct?" she asked the salesclerk. "That seems terribly high."

"Not at all," the clerk said. "This shawl is made from the finest vicuna wool in the world. No other wool is this soft and silky. It comes from high in the Andes. Each year there is only enough to make two dozen shawls. Feel it, please. Isn't that the most beautiful yarn in the world?"

"Yes, it is," said the customer, "and you certainly do tell it well, too."

107, 246, 526, 647, 678, 679, 761.

BARTENDER

73. A man rushed into a bar and ordered a double martini. The man downed it with one swallow, put a five dollar bill on the bar, and turned and rushed out of the bar.

The bartender picked up the five dollar bill, and folded it carefully and tucked it in his vest pocket. Just at that moment he looked up at the boss standing in the doorway staring at him.

Doing a bit of fast thinking he said, "Hi boss, did you see that fellow just now. Came in here, bought a double martini, gave me a five dollar tip, and rushed out without paying."

74. A man ordered a drink at a bar. His bill came to $1.45. The bartender gave the man a half dollar and a nickel in change. The man picked up the half dollar, left the nickel, and walked out of the bar.

"Well," said the bartender, "You win some and you lose some. That time I gambled and lost."

BASEBALL

75. The kindergarten teacher was teaching the children how to count and do simple arithmetic problems. "Johnny," she said, "can you tell me what is one and one?"

"That," said the little fellow, who had learned a lot by watching television, "means one ball and one strike."

76. A woman dropped in on her neighbor one afternoon to find her watching the baseball game on television. "I didn't know you were a baseball fan," she said.

"I'm not," the woman said, "but Bill just went to the store to get some beer and while he's gone, I'm the designated watcher."

77. The back door slammed and the little boy came into the kitchen, threw his baseball glove down on the floor and stood there on the verge of tears. "What in the world is the matter?" his mother asked. "Did you lose the game?"

"Worse than that," the little fellow sobbed, "I was traded."

"Now, now," his mother said. "That's all a part of the game. Sometimes even the world's greatest baseball stars are traded. Why should being traded upset you so?"

"Because," the little boy said, "I was traded for Harry's six year old sister."

78. The baseball fan was chatting over the back fence with his neighbor, who was a big league umpire. "Well, the season starts in two weeks," the man said. "Who's going to win the World Series this year?"

"Your guess is as good as mine," the umpire said.

"I've known that for years," the man said, "but this is the first time I ever heard you admit it."

319, 745.

BATH

79. The little girl came home from school and said to her mother, "I wish you would let me take my bath in the morning before I go to school instead of at night before I go to bed."

"What difference does it make?" her mother asked.

"Every day at school," the little girl said, "the teacher tells everybody to stand up who had a bath today. And I haven't even been able to stand up one time since school started."

BEAUTY

80. "My girl friend really isn't very pretty," a fellow said to his friend.

"I thought you told me she was a pin-up girl," his friend said.

"She is," the fellow said, " in a bowling alley."

81. A beautiful blonde was the center of attention of most of the men at a cocktail party. Half a dozen of them were standing as close as possible to her, and all of them were laughing and enjoying themselves.

On the other side of the room, a woman whispered to her husband, "Look at those men gathered round that blonde. I certainly don't see what the attraction is, do you?"

"No, I don't; so, I think I'll go take a closer look," he said as he sauntered across the room.

BEHAVIOR

82. A little boy was visiting his grandmother for the day. They talked of many things, and among other topics they chatted about spanking.

"You are a nice little boy," Grandmother said. "Does you father have to spank you very often?"

"Oh," said the little fellow, "now that I have started school he doesn't spank me anymore."

"He doesn't?" said Grandmother. "What does he do?"

"He just talks to me when I have misbehaved," the little boy said.

"What does he say?" Grandmother asked.

"I don't know," said the kid. "I never listen."

60, 650.

BELIEF

83. No matter how carefully they are explained, there are two things that people find hard to believe—how a man got a black eye and how a secretary got a mink coat.

587.

BIRTH CONTROL

84. Did it ever occur to you that everyone in the world who is in favor of birth control has already been born?

85. A well known politician was being interviewed on television. As usual, the interviewer asked questions about various subjects: taxes, international trade, law and order, food stamps and the energy crisis. Finally, he asked this question: "What do you think about birth control?"

"I'm glad you asked that question," the politician said, "because whenever anybody mentions the subject I always remind myself that I have three brothers and two sisters older than I am."

BIRTHDAY

86. A man wanted to be nice to his aunt on her ninetieth birthday; so he sent her a bottle of champagne and a small jar of caviar with this note attached: "Happy birthday. Live it up."

A week later he received a thank you note that said, "Thank you for remembering me on my birthday. I certainly did enjoy the gingerale—it was the best I ever drank. But the blackberry jam had spoiled. I think somebody must have stored it next to some fish."

87. A boy was trying hard to think of something to buy for his girlfriend. Finally, he asked his mother for a bit of guidance. "If you were going to be 16 years old tomorrow, what would you want?"

"Not another thing," his mother said without hesitation.

88. One Monday morning at breakfast a man said to his wife, "I think this is the first time in five or six years that I have remembered a special date. Thursday will be your birthday. How times flies. You'll be 40 years old. What would you like most?"

"Not to be reminded of it," was her quick reply.

89. The five-year-old was excited about her birthday party. "I hope I get lots and lots of presents at my party this afternoon," she said.

"It is not nice to think about getting," her mother said. "You should learn that true happiness comes from thinking about giving."

"All right," the little girl said, "I hope all my friends give me lots and lots of presents this afternoon."

90. A man who had reached his hundredth birthday was asked by a friend, "Of course, you can't drive anymore or get around as much as you used to. Are there any other disadvantages to being a hundred years old?"

"Only one that I can think of," the old man said, "it upsets me to see my grandchildren reaching middle age."

367, 420, 682, 737, 801.

BIRTHS

91. As three men were sitting restlessly in the hospital waiting room, a nurse rushed in and said to one of them, "Good news, your wife just had twins."

"What a coincidence," the man shouted. "I'm a ball player. I'm with the Minnesota Twins."

A few minutes later she returned and said to one of the other men, "My, what good news we are having today. Your wife just gave birth to triplets."

"Now *there's* a coincidence," the man said, "I work for the 3 M Company."

Just then the third man fainted. The nurse called an intern, and together they worked to revive the man. As a matter of routine, they checked his wallet for identification. It was then they they discovered that he was a salesman for 7-Up.

BLIND DATE

92. A college boy was arranging a blind date for his roommate.

"This is my cousin," he said. "You'll like her. She's five feet two, 19 years old, very pretty, and a good dancer. Let me tell you about her. She did weigh 135 pounds, but she made up her mind she was going to lose weight. At the same time, she gave up smoking. That was six months ago. Today she still doesn't smoke and she weighs only 105 pounds."

"She must be great," his roommate said, "but I had rather date a girl that doesn't have that much will power."

BOAT

93. Two men who were vacationing at Miami Beach had rented an outboard speed boat for a week. After running it up and down the bay for a few days, they figured they knew enough about it to take it into open water, which they did. About a mile off Miami Beach in the Atlantic Ocean, the motor went dead. Before they knew it they had drifted and were blown out of sight of land. However, they were pretty sharp, and after tinkering for a while, they had the motor running again. Only now they couldn't see land and didn't know which way to go. About that time a ship came by and they hailed it and asked the helmsman, "Which way to Miami Beach?"

The man shouted back, "Just a minute and I'll get you an exact solar reading."

The man in the little boat shouted, "Don't bother getting technical, just point."

548.

BOOK

94. A man was visiting a local author and book lover. The author's den and living room were filled with books, many of them stacked on the floor because of a lack of shelf space.

"You sure have a lot of books," the visitor said. "You've almost run out of shelves to put them on."

The author looked at him with a sheepish grin and said, 'That's because it's a lot easier to borrow books than it is to borrow book shelves."

351, 665.

BOSS

95. The boss called in his assistant office manager and said, "You told the personnel director that you were absent from work yesterday because you were sick, is that right?"

"Yes, sir," the man said.

"Well," his boss shouted, "you didn't look very sick when I saw you at the race track yesterday afternoon! What do you have to say about that?"

"You should have seen me throwing up after the third race," the man said.

96. Two men who worked for a disagreeable boss were chatting when he passed them in the hallway and went into his office and shut the door.

"Boy, is he hard to get along with," the first man said. "I feel like going right into his office and telling him where he can get off—again."

"What do you mean, again?" his friend said. "Do you mean to tell me you have done that?"

"No," the first man said. "I said I felt like doing it again. I felt like doing it last week and the week before, and now I feel that way again."

747.

BRAGGING

97. The tourist from Florida was shopping in a California fruit market. Being a natural born tease, he picked up a beautiful honey-dew melon and said to the clerk, "Is this the largest watermelon you can grow in California?"

Without hesitation the clerk said, "Sir, if you don't mind. We would rather that you not handle the grapes."

98. The high school senior had been given a compact car for her graduation present and was chatting about it with a friend.

"How many will it hold?" her friend asked.

"It was designed to hold five passengers," the proud owner said, "but if they are real friendly you can get ten in it."

99. The man from Kansas was mistakenly bragging to a Texan about the size of the hail in his wheat field. "Why," he said, "we've had many a hail storm when the hail was as big around as a quarter."

"That's nothing," the Texan said. "Down here we have hail that varies in size from a dollar to a dollar and a half."

100. A man and his wife were traveling out West and stopped at a sign that said, "Echo Point."

"Try it," the woman said.

"I think it's silly, but I'll try it," her husband said. With that he shouted at the top of his voice, "Baloney!"

After a minute, he said, "See, nothing happened."

"Try it again," his wife said.

This time he shouted, "I'm the best looking man in the world."

And then the echo came back, "Baloney!"

52, 108, 356, 751.

BRAVERY

101. The driver of a big semi-rig stopped at a truck stop for supper. He ordered a hamburger, french fries, cheese cake and coffee. Just as his food was placed in front of him, half a dozen rough looking motorcycle riders stormed into the place. They immediately began to harass him. They grabbed his hamburger and french fries and divided them. One drank his coffee and another took his cheese cake. They jeered him with such remarks as "Yellow truck driver. Chicken semi-pusher. Big babysitter."

The truck driver never said a word. He got up quickly, paid his bill, and hurried out into the night. After he had driven away, one of the motorcycle gang shouted at the manager of the truck stop, "He sure wasn't much of a man was he?"

"No, he wasn't," the man said. "And he wasn't much of a truck driver either. He just ran over six motorcycles as he backed his rig out of the parking lot."

325, 392, 753.

BREAKFAST

102. The little girl was spending the summer with her grandmother. For breakfast the first morning her grandmother gave her a glass of orange juice, a bowl of cereal and a glass of milk.

"At home," the little girl said, "Mommy always has bacon and eggs for breakfast."

Her grandmother, willing to break her neck to please her little granddaughter, took away the cereal and went to work preparing a bacon and egg breakfast. When she put it before her granddaughter, the little girl said, "No thank you."

Now grandmother was getting upset, and she said, "What do you mean, 'no thank you.' You told me your mother always has bacon and eggs for breakfast."

"That's what I said. Mommy has bacon and eggs, but I eat cereal."

529, 627.

BRIBERY

103. A road contractor wanted to keep up his goodwill with a certain office holder and offered to give him a new automobile.

The office holder said, "Sir, the ethics of my office and my personal integrity would never allow me to accept such a gift."

"I can understand how you feel about that," the contractor said. "Instead of me giving you the automobile, suppose I sell it to you at a greatly reduced price—say for $25.00."

The office holder thought a moment and then said, "In that case, I'll take two."

BRIDE

104. A man had just eaten the first meal his bride had ever cooked for him. Now came the dessert, homemade pie. After taking a taste of it he said, "What kind of pie is this, peach or apple or apricot?"

"Can't you tell from the taste?" his bride asked.

"No, I can't," he said.

"Then," she wanted to know, "what difference does it make?"

105. "I prefer to wait on brides," the manager of the meat department told a friend. "They don't remember what the price of meat used to be."

106. The bride-to-be was making out the invitations for her wedding. Her mother noticed that she had not invited any of her unmarried friends. The list consisted entirely of married persons. When her mother asked her about it, she said, "Oh, if I invited a lot of unmarried friends, one of these days I'll have to return the favor and buy wedding presents for them. This way, all of our presents will be clear profit."

312, 410, 470, 821.

BRIDE AND GROOM

107. It was a childhood marriage. The bride was 16 and the groom was only 17. The parents of the boy were a bit unhappy about it, but they attended the wedding. As their son was repeating the vows and came to the part that said, "with all my worldy goods, I thee endow," his mother whispered to her husband, "Oh, my, there goes his motor-scooter."

BRIDGE

108. Four women were playing bridge and chatting.

One woman said, "My husband just returned from Paris. He brought me loads of perfume. Imagine, 24 bottles, six ounces in a bottle—at $50.00 an ounce. What a gift. But, I can't use it because I suddenly find I'm allergic to perfume."

"Allergies are terrible," one of the other women said. "My husband bought me a full length mink coat. Guess what? I can't wear it because I'm allergic to mink."

The third woman spoke up and said, "It's the same with me. My husband gave me this beautiful diamond bracelet. But, I can't wear it because I'm allergic to diamonds."

The fourth woman suddenly rushed to the bathroom where she threw up her lunch. "How awful," her friends said. "What caused you to get sick all at once?"

"I guess it's because I'm allergic to baloney," the woman said.

216.

BUREAUCRAT

109. A man walked into a government office and asked, "Is this headquarters for the war on poverty?"

"Yes it is," the bureaucrat said.

"I have come in to surrender," the man said.

808.

BURGLAR

110. Two burglars were working together. They took turns; one watching outside while the other entered the house and looted it. On this particular occasion, the inside man was wearing squeaky shoes. As he tried to tiptoe upstairs in one house, a voice shouted down at him. "Take off those shoes. I've told you a thousand times not to track dirt and mud upstairs. Go back down and take them off."

The burglar came outside and told his friend, "I couldn't rob that house. It was too much like home."

62, 792.

BUSINESS

111. A rather prosperous hardware dealer in a small town kept his accounts payable in a big brown envelope, his cash in a cigar box and his accounts due stuck on a spindle.

His son, who had just passed his CPA examination, was visiting him and said, "Dad, I don't see how you can run your business that way. There's no way in the world that you can tell how much profit you are making. Why don't you let me install a modern bookkeeping system for you?"

"I don't need it son," the old man said. "My father was a tenant farmer, and when he died all I had to my name was a pair of overalls and a pair of shoes. So, I moved off the farm and came into town. I worked hard and saved my money and finally started this hardware store. Today, your older brother is a lawyer and your sister is a magazine editor. You are a CPA. Your mother and I live in a nice home and we have two cars. I own this hardware store. And everything is paid for. Now, the way I figure, about my accounting system—when you add all that together and subtract for the overalls and shoes, everything else is profit."

112. A newspaperman was interviewing a number of businessmen in order to get an overall picture of the local business trend.

"And how has your business been the past year?" he asked the partners of a used car lot.

"About usual," said the first.

"That's right," the second partner said. "We've had our ups and downs all year."

After the newspaperman had left, the first man said to his partner, "Have you been holding out on me? Name one time this past year when we've had any ups."

113. A tourist stopped at a wayside stand to buy some fruit from a farmer. "How's business?" he asked.

"Well," said the farmer. "It hasn't been good enough to quit, and it hasn't been bad enough to quit. But, I'm getting old and I wish it would hurry up and get one way or the other."

69.

CAMPAIGN

114. In the heat of a campaign speech one man had called his opponent a liar and a thief. The next day the newspapers quoted him as saying, "My opponent would steal anything he could get his hands on except an empty beer can."

That night on a television panel show, one of the reporters asked him if he had really said that. "No," the candidate said, "I was misquoted by the newspapers this morning. What I really said was that my opponent would steal anything he could get his hands on *including* an empty beer can."

115, 167, 565, 569, 573, 803.

CANDIDATE

115. During the height of a political campaign, one of the candidates was going from house to house introducing himself and passing out his literature. As he stepped into a yard and walked toward a woman working in her flower garden, a huge German police dog suddenly bounded from around the edge of the house and headed toward him with a fierce growl. Instantly, he turned and ran. As he whizzed out of the yard, the woman shouted after him, "What are you running for?"

"Congress, 5th District," he cried. "Please vote for me."

116. A huge crowd had gathered to hear the various candidates speak at the Labor Day picnic. One aspiring office holder ended his speech by declaring, "I intend to go to the convention and run as a favorite son."

One spectator said to another, "That was the greatest unfinished sentence I ever heard."

117. The candidate and his wife finally arrived home late at night. When they had removed their shoes and fallen onto the living room couch almost exhausted, the candidate said, "Oh, am I tired. This has been some day. I am exhausted."

"Me, too," said his wife. "I can't remember when I've been so tired."

"You tired?" her husband said. "I'm the one who made seven speeches today. Why are you so tired?"

"Because," said his wife, "I had to listen to every one of them."

118. A man who had announced his candidacy for mayor was having lunch with his brother. "The incumbent has been there for eight years and he'll be hard to beat. But, I guess if you work hard enough you might unseat him. What are the principal issues in the campaign?"

"Issues?" the candidate asked. "Issues? There aren't any issues. That's just a good job. He's got it. I want it."

37, 115, 188, 804.

CANNIBAL

119. The cannibal chief was preparing to cook the missionary who had been captured the day before. "You shouldn't eat him," one of his advisors said. "He is a missionary—a religious man."

"That's the reason I'm doing it," the chief said. "I think my people should have a taste of religion."

256.

CAREER

120. A husband said to his wife, "I'm sure all three of our kids are going to be doctors because they never come when we call them."

562.

CENSUS

121. A census taker was covering the most remote corners of his assigned territory. As he drove down a country road he saw a sign, "Beware of the Dog." A few hundred yards farther down the road, he saw another sign that said the same thing. Then when he came to the gate and drove into the farmyard, there was still another sign, this one larger than the rest: "Beware of the Dog."

Afraid to get out of his car, he honked his horn. Almost at once a farmer stepped through the door of the barn, followed by a tiny three-pound poodle wagging his friendly little tail.

After he had finished his work with the farmer, the census taker said, "The signs say 'beware of the dog.' Is that the only dog you have? Is that the dog the signs are all about?"

"It sure is," the farmer said with a grin.

"But that little dog won't keep anybody away," the census taker said.

"That's right," the farmer said, "but those signs sure do."

122. A census taker had stopped at a house where there were a dozen or more children playing in the yard. He was filling in his form as he talked to the housewife when he came to this question: "How many children do you have?"

"Now, let's see," she said. "There's Alice, and Bertha, and Charles, and Donna, and . . . ."

"Excuse me," the census taker said. "I don't need their names. We're only interested in numbers."

"That's an insult!" screamed the woman. "We don't give our children numbers. We give them names."

123. The census taker had asked a backwoods woman how many children she had. Obviously too ignorant to know how to count, she said, "Well, let's see, I've got one school bus rider, one yard child, one porch child, one creeper, and one still on the bottle."

407.

CHAMBER OF COMMERCE

124. The anesthesiologist was consulting with his patient before an operation. "What would you prefer?" he asked, "ether, gas or chloroform?"

"Considering that I am the Secretary of the Chamber of Commerce," the patient said, "I think I should patronize local industry. So, how about giving me a local anesthetic."

CHANGE

125. A Broadway actress was suffering from nervous tension and strain. She went to a psychiatrist, and he told her she needed to get away from her normal routine. "You need a change," he said.

"A change?" she said. "In the past six years I have been in five different plays, have lived in seven different apartments, have been married to three different men, have owned nine cars and have traveled to 24 states and nine countries. What sort of change did you have in mind?"

594.

CHARITY

126. A woman was having a cup of coffee with her next door neighbor. "I feel real good today. I started this morning out with an act of unselfish generosity. I gave a five dollar bill to a bum."

"You mean you gave a bum five dollars? That's a lot of money to give away like that. What did your husband say about it?"

"Oh, he thought it was the thing to do. He said, 'Thanks.' "

CHEAP

127. The world's stingiest man went Christmas shopping, but everything he saw was too expensive except a $50.00 vase that was on sale for $2.00 because the handle had been broken off. He bought it and had the salesman ship it by mail so that his friend would think he had paid $50.00 for it and that it had been broken in shipment.

A week after Christmas he received a thank you note from his friend. "Thank you for the lovely vase," his letter said. "It was so nice of you to wrap each piece separately."

CHECK

128. A man and his wife have a joint checking arrangement. Whenever he calls to say he is working late and he doesn't get home by midnight, she starts checking the joints.

345.

CHILDREN

129. "How did school go today?" a mother asked her little boy.

"Fine," the little fellow said. "We had a new teacher and she wanted to know if I had any brothers and sisters and I told her I was an only child."

"What did she say?" his mother asked.

"She said, 'Thank goodness!' "

130. The little boy's mother had called him and four of his friends in from the back yard where they were playing. She seated them around the kitchen table and proceeded to open a large one-calorie bottle of diet cola.

One of the little fellows watched carefully as she filled each of the five glasses. Then he said, "I wonder which one of us got the calorie."

202, 253, 450, 546.

CHOICE

131. A young lady was chatting with a friend. "All I want in a husband is a man who is good looking, kind and understanding. And I don't think that is too much to expect from a millionaire."

132. "Elmer, aren't you getting hard of hearing lately?"

"Yes, I am," Elmer said. "And I went to see the doctor about it."

"What did he say?"

"He said if I didn't quit drinking so much I'd get as deaf as a post."

"Are you going to quit?"

"No," Elmer said. "I tried it two weeks. My hearing improved all right, but I went back to drinking because I liked what I was drinking more than what I was hearing."

133. A little boy became separated from his father at the State Fair. He eventually found himself in the hands of a friendly policeman who said he would have no trouble finding his father. "What's he like," the policeman asked.

"Fast cars and beer," the little fellow said without any hesitation.

134. Two men were drinking and chatting and kidding each other at a bar.

"You are a man of the world," the first man said. "You are an expert on wine, women and song. If you had to give up one of them, which would you give up?"

"Song," his friend said.

"Okay, if you then had to give up wine or women, which would you give up?"

After thinking a moment, his friend said, "That would depend on the vintage of each one."

23, 757.

CHRISTMAS

135. A little boy had received a toy drum for Christmas and was so pleased with it that he beat on it all day long. Hour after hour he beat on it as hard as he could. He was making nervous wrecks of everybody in the neighborhood. Nobody could stop him. His father and mother had tried to divert his attention to other gifts. His older sister had even threatened him. But, no! He kept on beating his little drum.

After about three days of drum beating, an uncle dropped by the house to wish everybody a happy holiday season. When he saw the problem, he said, "Don't worry, I'll fix it."

He jumped in his car and was gone for 15 minutes. When he returned, he said to the little boy, "I've got something for you in the car." He took him outside, put something in his hand and chatted with him for a few minutes. After that, the drum beating stopped. Complete silence.

"Wonderful," said the kid's dad. "What did you give him? What did you say to him?"

"Oh," said the boy's uncle. "I just went to the hardware store and bought him a scout knife. When I gave it to him I asked him if he had ever seen the 'boom-boom-fairies' who lived inside his drum."

136. During the Christmas shopping rush a mother visited a large toy department with her little five year old boy. As he entered the toy department he spotted a hobby horse and headed directly for it and climbed on. When it came time to move along, his mother couldn't get him off the hobby horse. She tried persuasion, she threatened, she promised him an ice cream cone, nothing worked. The kid wouldn't get off the hobby horse. She sought help. The head clerk, the Santa Claus on duty, the store manager, nobody could get him off the hobby horse. The mother even called the boy's father, who came from work to try. But he failed.

In desperation, they called the fire department. When the fire chief arrived, he took one look at the situation, walked over to the little boy on the hobby horse and whispered something in his ear. The little fellow said, "Yes, sir," and climbed down off the hobby horse.

"My, you're a genius with children," the mother said.

"Not really," the fire chief said. "I just told him to get off the hobby horse or I was going to bat his teeth down his throat."

137. A woman was telling her friend about Christmas at her house. "I was visited by a jolly, bearded fellow with a big bag over his shoulder. My son came home from college with his dirty laundry."

138. A man who lived in an apartment with valet parking called for his car one morning about two weeks before Christmas and took off for work. On the dashboard he noticed a colorful little greeting, fastened with tape, which read, "Merry Christmas from all the men in the garage."

He thought nothing about it until two days before Christmas when he found another card stuck in the same place. It read, "Merry Christmas from all the men in the garage—second notice."

139. A woman was shopping for a Christmas present for her five year old boy. She was fascinated with a new mechanical toy kit and said to the clerk, "Are you sure this isn't too complicated for a five year old boy?"

"It's all right for any age," the clerk said. "This is a modern educational toy designed to prepare a child for the frustrations and anxieties in today's world. No matter how he puts it together, it won't work."

140. A husband said to his wife, "What would you like for Christmas?"

"Nothing much," she said. "How about something you made yourself—like money?"

CHURCH

141. An eight year old boy from a small town was visiting his grandparents in the city. They were members of a church where the congregation was so large that the minister held three services each Sunday—at 9:30, 10:30 and 1:30.

At breakfast on Sunday morning, this was explained to the grandson. After some discussion it was decided that they would attend the 10:30 service.

As they entered the narthex of the huge church, the little boy noticed a large bronze plaque on the wall with dozens of names listed in alphabetical order.

"What is that?" the kid asked.

"That," said his grandfather, "is a memorial in honor of the men who died in the service."

"Which service," the kid wanted to know, "the 9:30, the 10:30 or the 1:30?"

142. The phone rang in the bank, and the voice said, "I'd like to speak to someone about bonds, please?"

"Conversion or redemption?" the switchboard operator asked.

"Excuse me," the voice said. "Do I have the First National Bank or the First Baptist Church?"

143. The old man was deaf as a post, but he wouldn't wear a hearing aid. He didn't seem to mind. His family wrote notes to him and he seemed well adjusted to his problem. Every Sunday morning he went to church even though he couldn't hear the singing, scripture reading or the sermon.

One day a friend wrote on a slip of paper, "Why do you bother to go to church when you can't hear anything?"

"Oh," the old man said, "I just want to be seen there. I want people to know which side I am on."

184, 465.

COFFEE

144. "This coffee is terrible," the customer said. "What kind is it?"

"It's blended coffee," the waitress said.

"Blended?" the customer asked. "What kind of blend?"

"Last week's and this week's," the waitress said.

126, 540, 617. 625.

COLLEGE

145. The young college girl wrote this letter to her mother:

"Dear Mother: Everything is going fine at school. I met the most wonderful young man I've ever known. He is a junior. He plays football, is studying to be a doctor, makes excellent grades and is tall and handsome. I have had eight dates with him and have worn all eight of my dresses. Now, I need something to wear next week because he has invited me to go to the theatre with him. Will you please send $25.00 for a new dress?"

Her mother replied, "No need for any new clothes. Find a new boyfriend and start all over."

756.

COLLEGE BOY

146. A young man who had been hired by the personnel department of a large supermarket chain reported to work at one of the stores. The manager greeted him with a warm handshake and a smile, handed him a broom and said, "Your first job will be to sweep out the store."

"But," the young man said, "I'm a college graduate."

"I'm sorry," the manager said. "I didn't know that. Here, give me the broom and I'll show you how."

147. A college boy was chatting with a classmate. "You look down in the dumps. What happened, did you flunk a course?"

"Oh, no," his friend said. "Suddenly, I feel as though I have been betrayed. I wrote home for money to buy a study desk and guess what—my folks sent me a study desk."

148. At last we have found the laziest person in the world—a college boy who is too lazy to write home for money.

149. A man was chatting with a friend. "I don't know what to do about my son. He's been away to college two years now and he hasn't learned to drink or play cards."

"Gee," said his friend. "You're lucky. Why in the world do you want him to learn to drink and play cards?"

"Because," said the first man, "he drinks and plays cards."

150. Two mothers were chatting. "I think my son is home from college," the first mother said.

"What do you mean, you think he is home?" her friend said. "If you haven't seen him, what makes you think he is home?"

"Because," said the first mother, "we haven't had a letter from him asking for money for more than two weeks—and besides, the car is gone."

151. The college boy met a girl at a football game and asked her for a date.

"I'm sorry," she said, "but I never go out with perfect strangers."

"That's fine," he said. "Let's go. I'm far from perfect."

17, 137, 297, 593.

COMMITTEE

152. Did you ever see a committee of five work? One man does all the work; two men tell him how to do it; one man pats him on the back for doing it well; and the fifth man keeps the minutes of the meetings.

* * * * * *

A committee is an organized group that keeps minutes and wastes hours.

* * * * * *

Search all your parks in all your cities;
You'll find no statues to committees.

153. You can always spot the newest member of a committee. He is the fellow who arrived on time.

* * * * * *

A committee is a group of the unknowledgeable, assigned by the unwilling and unprepared to figure out an unworkable way to do the unnecessary.

* * * * * *

A committee does its most effective work when it consists of onlv three members—two of whom are absent.

154. If Columbus had been a committee, they would still be arguing whether or not the world was flat.

* * * * * *

A kangaroo is an animal that looks as though he had been put together by a committee.

* * * * * *

A committee meetıng is a group of people talking about a problem that they should be working on.

* * * * * *

A committee is a group of people with a problem that they can't solve individually—meeting to decide that nothing needs to be done about it anyway.

315.

COMMUNICATION

155. A salesman called on a machine shop in a small town and asked for the manager.

The young lady at the front desk said, "Go through that door marked 'Employees Only' and turn to the right. Go up the stairs and you'll find a door marked 'No Admittance. This Means You.' Go through there and down the hall to a door with a sign on it 'Quiet, Men At Work.' That's the machine shop. If the machines are running, you'll have to yell for him. His name is Wilbur."

156. The explorer heard the sound of drums coming from deep within the jungle. So in the spirit of discovery he slashed his way through the thicket in search of the drums. At last he came to a clearing where a witch doctor of a strange tribe was beating on a hollow log.

Through his native interpreter, the explorer said to the witch doctor, "Why doctor make boom-boom?"

"We need water—we want water," the witch doctor said.

"So," the explorer said, "witch doctor beat drum for rain?"

The interpreter didn't bother to translate that question. Instead, he turned to the explorer and said, "Don't be silly. He's calling the plumber."

157. A housewife woke up the other morning with a severe case of laryngitis. For four days she couldn't even whisper. To help her communicate without wasting time writing notes, her husband set up a clever arrangement. She would tap on the table when she wanted to say something. One tap meant "yes," two taps meant "no," three taps meant "what would you like for supper," and so on. Eighty-seven taps meant "take out the garbage."

158. A clerk was trying to sell a man some shaving lotion. "This will attract the girls," he said. "It smells like a credit card."

159. The tourist driving down a country road came face to face with a sign which said, "Road Closed—Do Not Enter." The road ahead looked pretty good to him, and having had great experience as a traveler, he ignored the sign and pressed on.

Five miles down the road he came to a bridge that was out and he had to turn around and retrace his route. As he reached the point where the warning sign stood, he read the words printed on his side of it. "Welcome back, stupid."

160. A customer was buying a fountain pen. To be sure he had exactly the point that suited him best, he tried out half a dozen or so by writing on a scratch pad. Each time he would write the words "E Pluribus Unum."

The clerk who was waiting on him was trying to be helpful, and finally she said, "Here are three more pens with gold points, Mr. Unum. Maybe one of these will be just what you are looking for."

161. A sales manager who was considered an expert at staging sales seminars was giving some advice to his new assistant.

"One temptation I must warn you against," he said. "As you are conducting a sales meeting you will often find people will disagree with some of your ideas. You sometimes see someone shaking his head as you speak. Now, the natural thing for you to do is to take out after that fellow and try to convince him. Don't do it. Because, the chances are that he's the only person listening to you."

162. When the man answered the telephone a voice said, "When are you coming over? We've been waiting at Joe's house for an hour."

Thinking the call might be for one of his teenage children the man said, "To whom did you wish to speak?"

"Sorry," the voice said, "I'm sure I've got the wrong number. Nobody I know says 'whom.' "

163. The phone rang and the receptionist said, "Ringo, Murphy and Wilson."

"Good morning," the caller said. "Is Mr. Murphy there?"

"May I say who is calling?" the receptionist asked.

"Yes," the caller said. "This is Pickens, Perkins and Peller. Mr. Pickens calling."

"Just a moment, I'll connect you," she said.

"Hello, this is Mr. Murphy's office." his secretary said.

"Mr. Pickens is calling Mr. Murphy," the caller said, "Will you put Mr. Murphy on, please?"

"Mr. Murphy is here," the secretary said, "Will you put Mr. Pickens on, please?"

"Mr. Pickens?" the voice said. "Ready with Mr. Murphy."

"Hi, Gene, this is Curtis," Pickens said. "How about lunch today and then we'll play golf this afternoon. Okay?"

"Okay," Murphy said. "I'll see you at the clubhouse dining room at twelve o'clock."

8, 93, 123, 352, 453, 549, 608, 740, 749, 759, 774.

COMPLAINT

164. A shopper had returned a blouse to the department store and was arguing with the clerk about it. "I want my money back. Just look at this blouse I bought last week."

"What's the matter with it?" the clerk asked.

"It faded. You told me the colors were fast," she said. "And the very first time it was washed, it faded."

"That sure was fast, wasn't it?" the clerk said.

251, 258, 289, 620, 680.

COMPUTER

165. The businessman dragged himself home and barely made it to his easy chair before he dropped exhausted. His sympathetic wife was right there with a tall cool drink and a comforting word.

"My, you look tired," she said. "You must have had a hard day today. What happened to make you so exhausted?"

"It was terrible," her husband said. "The computer broke down and all of us had to do our own thinking."

360, 488, 787.

CONFUSION

166. The new tenant in an apartment house inadvertently got off on the wrong floor and put his key into what he thought was his apartment door. As he shook the door and struggled with the key a man came up behind him and said, "Can I help you?"

"No," the first man said. "It's this darn lock, it seems to be stuck."

"Well," the man said, "if it becomes unstuck and if that key opens that door, both you and my wife have a lot of explaining to do."

232, 440, 709

CONGRESSMAN

167. Two men were running for Congress. One was obviously a scalawag who was making a lot of wild campaign promises. The other was a pillar of the community, a fine upright citizen.

A woman voter who detested the first man voted for him anyway. Her husband asked her why. "Well," she said, "everybody knows that politics ruins people. They may not be bad when they go into office, but they certainly are ruined by the time they leave office. And I didn't see any reason to ruin a good man."

168. Ask almost any congressman about government waste and he'll begin to tell you about some money that the government is spending in some other congressman's district.

169. The Labor Day picnic was at its height. The congressman was shaking hands with everyone and being the hail-fellow-well-met. Everyone was there, high society and the working class. Among those present was the congressman's tailor. He came up to the congressman and shook his hand. The congressman said, "I recognize you, but for the moment I can't recall your name."

The tailor leaned over and whispered in the congressman's ear, "I made your pants."

"Oh, yes," the congressman said. "Now I remember you. I want you to meet some friends of mine." And turning to another group standing nearby he said, "I want you to meet a long time friend of mine, Major Pants."

170. The newly elected congressman was holding his first press conference. A reporter from a newspaper that had opposed the congressman tried to embarrass him with a question. "Sir, when you go to Washington, will you give in to the powerful forces that everyone knows control you?"

"The congressman had a ready reply, "I would appreciate it if you would confine your questions strictly to questions pertaining to my congressional office and not about my wife."

115, 566, 571, 614, 803.

CONSCIENCE

171. The teacher asked her pupils, "Everybody has a conscience. Can anybody tell me what that means? Can anybody give me a definition of 'conscience'?"

One little fellow said, "When you break something, that's what makes you tell you mother before your sister does."

397, 487.

CONSERVATION

172. A man became lost down a country road and stopped at a farm house to ask directions. He found the farmer on his back porch filling half a dozen lamps and trimming the wicks.

The man said he was surprised to see the farmer still using lamps in the house. "Why don't you have electricity wired into your home?"

"Oh, we have electricity," the farmer said, "but we've never had to use it because we have never run out of kerosene yet."

173. The boy's father was giving him a bad time over his report card. "Now we come to this figure," the father said. "Here is a 64. Now how did that happen?"

Never quite willing to throw in the towel, the boy said, "Maybe it's the new setting for the thermostat because of the energy crisis—maybe?"

CONTRIBUTION

174. A man running for office was trying to raise campaign funds by mail. To be sure that everyone in his district was reached, he sent a mass mailing addressed to "Occupant."

A few days later he received a check in the mail for $5,000. It was signed "Occupant."

175. The principal speaker at a United Givers fund-raising dinner said to the orchestra leader, "As I come to the end of my speech tonight, I am going to call on everyone in the audience who will pledge $100 to stand up. At exactly that moment, I want your orchestra to play some appropriate music."

"What music," the orchestra leader asked, "would you consider appropriate?"

"Why," said the speaker, "The Star Spangled Banner, of course."

249, 342.

CONVENTION

176. Two women had met at a convention where their husbands were attending all-day meetings. They had spent the morning together, shopping, relaxing by the swimming pool, and walking up and down the beach. When it came time for lunch, one of the women said, "Before we go to lunch, would you like to have a cocktail?"

"No, thank you," her new made friend said, "I never drink."

"Oh," said the first woman, "is it a matter of religion?"

"No," said her friend. "My husband and I have an agreement never to drink in front of the children. And when I'm away from them, who needs a drink?"

CONVERSATION

177. A man had just installed his first CB radio in his car and was trying it out as he drove down a country road. After he had fiddled with switches and dials and shouted into his microphone for 10 or 15 minutes with no results, his wife said to him, "If you are so desperate to communicate with someone, how about if you quit fooling with that thing and talk to me?"

295, 617, 711.

COURAGE

178. A man spoke to a fellow sitting next to him at a bar. "What do you do for a living?"

"I work for a carnival. I'm a human cannonball."

"Hey, I never met a human cannonball before. I'll bet your job takes a lot of courage."

"It sure does," the cannonball said. "That's why I'm here right now. I have to get loaded before I can do it."

239.

CREDIT

179. A man who was head over heels in debt received this note from one of his creditors: "Dear Sir: Please pay something on your account. We have been extremely patient with you. In fact, we have done more for you than your mother did. We have carried you for eleven months."

180. The credit manager had tried for months to collect from the town's worst deadbeat. The only reply he got was, "Quit pestering me."

At that, the credit manager gave what he considered the ultimate threat. "Pay me something on your account today or I'll call your other creditors and tell them that you have paid me in full. Then see how you'll be pestered."

181. Two credit managers were comparing the credit ratings of their customers. "Oh, yes," said one of them, "what about this fellow Pickens. How trustworthy is he?"

"We don't know," the other credit man said. "He always pays cash so we have no way of knowing how reliable he is."

736.

CRITIC

182. A young playwright gave a special invitation to a highly regarded critic to watch his new play. The critic came to the play but slept through the entire performance.

The young playwright was indignant and said, "How could you sleep when you knew how much I wanted your opinion?"

"Young man," the critic said, "sleep is an opinion."

531, 700, 701, 703.

CURE

183. A man was complaining to a friend about his inability to sleep.

"What do you take when you can't sleep?" he asked his friend.

"I always drink a glass of wine or a martini at regular intervals," his friend said.

"Will that make you sleep?"

"No," his friend said, "but it makes me satisfied to stay awake."

184. A man visited his doctor to ask if he could help him with his problem of snoring. "As soon as I go to sleep," the man said, "I start to snore. Every time. What can I do to cure myself?"

"Does it bother your wife?" the doctor asked.

"Oh," the man said, "it not only bothers her but it disturbs the entire congregation."

13, 292, 596, 611, 828.

CUSTOMER

185. The shoe salesman had shown the woman more than 25 pairs of shoes before she finally settled on the first pair she had tried on. As she paid for her purchase and was leaving the store, he said to her, "Thank you for coming. I wish I had a dozen customers like you."

One of the other clerks heard him and when the customer had gone, said, "You told her you wished you had a dozen customers like her. Why did you say that to such an overbearing and hard to please person?"

"Because it's true," the salesman said. "I have a hundred like her and I wish I only had a dozen."

680.

CUSTOMS

186. As the airline passenger was returning to the United States, the officer at customs asked him if he had anything to declare. "Nothing in the bag except my clothing," the man said.

"I have to make a check," the officer said. So he opened the man's bag and found a bottle of rum wrapped in an undershirt.

"What about this?" the officer demanded. "You told me you had nothing in your bag except clothing."

"Right," the man said. "That is my nightcap."

DEAFNESS

187. Uncle John's hearing had begun to deteriorate and the doctor recommended a hearing aid. Thinking they were far too expensive, Uncle John merely inserted an ear plug from a portable radio and fastened the end of the connecting wire underneath his necktie where it was out of sight.

One of his friends knew what he had done and said to him, "That's not connected to anything. How can that help you to hear?"

"Oh, you'd be surprised," Uncle John said. "Now, when anybody sees that they talk louder."

132, 352.

DEBATE

188. The incumbent was an old experienced campaigner of the rough and tumble school of politics. As he was preparing for a face-to-face television debate with his opponent, his staff appeared to be nervous.

"Don't worry," the old-timer told them, "I'll take care of him with an embarrassing question."

"But we've researched his past and can't find a single embarrassing incident," his chief assistant said.

"That's no problem," the old timer said. "I'll just ask him what he was doing in Atlantic City on the night of May 5, 1946."

"What was he doing that night? Was he *really* there?" his assistant wanted to know.

"I don't know where he was and neither does he," said the old-timer. "So, he'll deny that he was there. And the more he denies it, the more suspicious his denials will sound. The newspapermen will ask him that same question everytime he has a press conference. The mystery of Atlantic City will become the biggest issue of the campaign—and his unwillingness to come clean will defeat him. Come on, let's get over to the television station and get it over with."

DELAY

189. A housewife was getting some clothes ready to give to the Goodwill. Just to be safe, she was looking through the pockets of everything to see if there was something someone had forgotten. Sure enough, in a five year old sport jacket she found a shoe repair ticket.

She was sure that after five years the shoes had been disposed of, but she thought she'd check anyway. The next morning she took the ticket to the shoe repairman and, sure enough, still on the shelf were her shoes. She said to the man, "Here is the ticket for those shoes. I'll just take them with me."

The repairman checked the number of the ticket with the ticket on the shoes and said, "Yes, that's the right ticket, all right, but the shoes won't be ready until Friday."

DENTIST

190. A mother was sitting in the dentist's reception room with her four year old daughter. While they were waiting for their appointment, a patient left the dentist's inner sanctum and walked through the lobby and out the front door. He was a young man with long hair and a full beard. He was wearing a golden robe that hid everything except his bare feet. Around his neck were half a dozen strings of beads and three small bells that tinkled as he walked.

As the office door closed behind him, the little girl whispered to her mother, "Was that the tooth fairy?"

538.

DEPENDABILITY

191. The young man was filling in his application for employment, including his tax withholding forms. After the question that asked about his dependents he marked the box that said "No."

"Aren't you married?" the personnel man asked. "If so, you are supposed to mark the box that says 'Yes.' "

"Yes," the young man said, "I'm married, but my wife isn't dependable."

812.

DETECTIVE

192. A jealous husband hired a private detective to spy on his wife. "I am sure she has a boyfriend," he said, "and I want evidence for a divorce."

After several weeks, the detective reported to the man and brought photographic evidence. "Here is everything you need," the detective said. "This picture shows them having a picnic at the beach together. And this one shows them dancing at the country club and this one hugging and kissing in a car parked by the airport."

"I can't believe it," the husband said. "I just can't believe it."

"But, it's all there in the pictures," the detective said.

"Oh, I can see that, all right," the husband said. "What I can't believe is that she could be having that much fun."

615.

DIET

193. A secretary joined a friend of hers in a sandwich shop. The first girl had ordered her lunch and was nibbling on a cottage cheese sandwich. "Are you on some sort of low calorie diet?" the first girl asked.

"Not a low calorie diet," her friend said. "I'm on a low salary diet."

194. The woman was about 60 pounds overweight, and the doctor had been advising her for severals months about her problem. No matter what sort of diet he would prescribe, she just wouldn't stick to it. Finally, one day he said to her, "We've tried everything I can think of to get your weight down, but you won't follow my directions. I have only one suggestion left. Why don't you forget about dieting and learn to be jolly."

195. The doctor had prescribed a reducing diet for a 200 pound patient. "Your health is in danger unless you lose weight. So, stick to this diet—absolutely. And six months from now I want to see three-fourths of you back here for a checkup."

196. A mother was urging her little boy to eat everything on his plate. "Now eat your spinach," she said. "It will put color in your cheeks."

"Maybe so," he said, "but who wants green cheeks?"

197. Little Willy's idea of a balanced meal is a hot dog in one hand and a coke in the other.

* * * * * *

Remember: You can't lose weight by talking about it. You've got to keep your mouth shut.

198. A woman was telling her friend about her diet. "It's the world's greatest weight-reducing diet. From noon on Friday until breakfast the following Friday, all you have is grapefruit juice. Nothing else. When you get hungry, drink a glass of grapefruit juice."

"Does it work?" her friend asked.

"It certainly does. It does two things. It makes you lose about ten pounds and teaches you to hate grapefruit juice."

199. "You look a lot thinner than the last time I saw you," a man said to his friend. "Are you on some special kind of diet to lose weight?"

"Oh, no," his friend said. "I'm losing this weight because of the worries that my new tax consultant is causing me."

"In that case," the man said, "why don't you fire him and hire somebody else?"

"Oh, I'm going to do that," his friend said, "just as soon as he worries eight more pounds off of me."

92, 314.

DISCIPLINE

200. Two mothers were chatting about their children and the problems of raising them in today's precarious world.

"My three boys stick together," the first woman said. "They are loyal to each other. When one of them misbehaves, the other won't tell on him."

"Well then," the other woman asked, "how do you ever find out which one to punish?"

"It's not too hard," the first mother said. "When one of them gets into mischief, we send all three of them to bed without their supper. Then, the next morning we paddle the one with the black eye."

82, 269.

DIVORCE

201. The judge was questioning a woman about her suit for divorce. "Do you mean to say that you want to divorce your husband merely because he is careless about his appearance?"

"Yes," the woman said. "He hasn't made an appearance at home in more than two years."

202. Two long-time friends were chatting. "I'm so glad to see that you decided not to get a divorce," the first woman said.

"Yes," said her friend. "We decided to stay together because of the children. George wouldn't take them and neither would I."

203. The judge was talking to the woman who wanted a divorce. "You say in your complaint that you want to divorce your husband on grounds of poor health. Would you please explain what you mean."

"It's very simple, your honor. I got sick of having him around the house."

204. A woman was suing for divorce on the grounds that her husband was an alcoholic.

"This is a strange case," the judge said. "You've only been married three months. Didn't you know before you married him that your husband drank heavily?"

"No, your honor, I didn't," she said. "I didn't discover it until one night when he came home sober."

205. An attorney in a divorce case was questioning the wife. "Isn't it true that your husband led a dog's life?"

"He certainly did," she said. "He always came into the house covered with mud and left his footprints all over the house. Then, he'd settle down in the most comfortable chair in the house—the one nearest the fireplace. Once he got confortable he sat there scratching and yelling for something to eat. He growled at the least provocation and snapped at me a dozen times every evening. And that's exactly why I want to divorce him."

416, 630.

DOCTOR

206. A doctor and a lawyer ate lunch in the same restaurant every day and both of them fell in love with the cashier. The rivalry between the two became intense. Then one day the lawyer was called out of town on business. Before he left he said to the cashier, "I'm going to be out of town for ten days and I would like you to have this little gift."

When she opened it she found ten bright red apples.

207. The doctor asked his eighty year old patient how he was feeling.

"Well," the old fellow said, "I'm still kicking, but I'm not raising as much dust as I used to."

208. A man took the morning off from work to have his annual physical checkup at the local clinic. As usual, the doctor pronounced him in good shape, except that his blood pressure and cholesterol count were a bit high. Even though the examination cost was more than $100, the man felt good about the results.

When he left the clinic, he hailed a taxi to take him back to work. The driver said, "I pick up a lot of people at the clinic. Did you go there for a checkup?"

"Yes, I did," the man said.

"You look like a healthy businessman," the driver said. "Probably nothing wrong with you except maybe your blood pressure and cholesterol count are too high."

209. A doctor was explaining to his young assistant, "When a man comes in with nervous stomach I ask him if he plays golf. If he says 'yes,' I advise him to stop. If he says 'no,' I advise him to start."

210. A young doctor was complaining to an older colleague, "Every time I attend the weekly meeting of my service club somebody gets me in the corner and starts pumping me for free medical advice. It's embarrassing, but I don't know how to prevent it."

"No problem," the old timer said. "I figured that one out years ago. When anyone does that to me, I stop him with one word—'undress.' "

211. Like most people, a surgeon was upset and a bit irate about the high cost of having his car repaired.

"This is ridiculous," he said, "Four hundred and twenty dollars for grinding the valves and putting in new rings. Your price is way out of line."

"Not really, when you think about it," the garage owner said. "You are a surgeon, and you should realize that an automobile engine is just as complicated as a human body. The mechanic who worked on your car has to be just as skilled at his job as you do."

"In that case," the surgeon said, "I'd like to see him grinding valves while the engine is running."

212. The doctor was talking to his patient about the necessity of an operation. "You are going to need the operation and you shouldn't put it off."

"How much will it cost?" the man asked.

"Counting the hospital bill and everything," the doctor said, "it will cost about $5,400."

"This is terrible," the man said, "because I just don't have that kind of money in cash."

"Could you pay me so much a month?" the doctor asked.

"I'm sure I could manage that," the man said.

The doctor said, "Fine. Could you pay $142.50 a month?"

"Yes," the man said, "I could do that. That amount sounds funny though. It's just like buying a car."

"I am," the doctor said.

213. After the doctor had examined his patient, he asked her to sit in the chair beside his desk and stick out her tongue. He then proceeded to write out two prescriptions. When he had finished he said, "Ah, yes, that is fine. You may shut your mouth."

With that, he thanked her for coming, told her she would be all right, and escorted her to the door.

When he had shut the door behind the patient, his nurse said to him, "Why did you have her sitting there for five minutes with her tongue sticking out? You never even looked at it."

"That was just to keep her quiet so I could concentrate while I wrote out her prescriptions," he said.

214. Several hundred doctors and their wives were attending a formal banquet. The speaker of the evening was a distinguished physician who weighed in the neighborhood of 280 pounds. When his speech was over and he sat down, his chair collapsed. As he was struggling to his feet, a voice called out, "Is there a carpenter in the house?"

215. Doctor: "You should take a warm bath before retiring."

Patient: "How can that help me now? I don't retire for another 16 years."

216. The doctor was giving the patient his annual physical. He noticed that the man's shins were rather badly bruised, and he said to him jokingly, "What do you play, hockey, or soccer, or lacrosse?"

"None of those," the man said. "The only game I play is bridge."

217. The young doctor had just opened an office in his home town. One of his first patients was his father. "You ought to be ashamed of yourself," the old man said to his son. "I worked and sweated and sacrificed and did without the pleasures of life so that you could go to school and be a doctor. And the first thing you do when you get back home is to tell me I have to give up smoking."

218. It was 2:00 A.M. in the middle of a snowstorm when the doctor's phone rang. "You've got to come at once," the voice on the phone said. "My wife is having some kind of an attack and is in terrible pain."

"I have had a terrible night," the doctor said. "I've only had one hour's sleep because my car is stuck in a snow bank and I had to walk two miles home. But, I'll get dressed and see what I can do for your wife. The only thing is, I don't have any transportation. You'll have to come and get me."

"What?" the man shouted. "You expect me to go out in this kind of weather?"

219. A doctor had worked hard to send his son to the finest medical schools. His pride knew no bounds when his son finished his internship and announced that he was coming back home to work with his father.

The first day on the job he suggested that his father and mother take a trip to Europe. "You have worked hard all your life and you need a vacation. I am sure I can handle the practice while you are gone."

That sounded wonderful, and so the doctor and his wife took their trip. Six weeks later when they returned, the doctor asked how things had gone.

"Everything ran smoothly. Just the routine things. I delivered three babies, and had one case of appendicitis. Probably the best thing I was able to do was cure Mrs. Twigg's bronchitis. It had plagued her for years, but I found a new antibiotic that cleared it up in two weeks."

"My goodness," his father said, "you sure messed up a good thing. It was Mrs. Twigg's cough that paid your way through school and took care of the expenses for our trip to Europe."

220. Three senior citizens were chatting about this and that and their health.

"What would you do," the first one asked, "if your doctor told you that you had only six months to live?" He then answered his own question by saying, "As for me, I'd travel. I'd cash in everything I own and spend those six months taking a trip around the world."

"I'd do pretty much the same thing," the second man said. "I'd cash in all of my stocks and bonds, but instead of traveling around the world, I'd travel around the United States and visit my four children and their families and see some of my old friends."

The first man looked at the third fellow and asked, "What would you do?"

"The first thing I'd do," he said, "would be to go see another doctor."

221. Some women were playing bridge and chatting. One of them was bragging about her doctor. "He's absolutely marvelous. He's young and tall and dark and handsome and he takes care of all my aches and pains. He knows exactly what's wrong with me and always prescribes exactly the right medicine. You should go to him."

"But," said one of the women, "I don't need to go to a doctor—there's nothing the matter with me."

"Oh, but my doctor is so wonderful," said the first woman, "he'll find something."

222. A hospital intern who had been assigned to the maternity ward was talking to a friend. "I have finally found my calling," he said. "I am going to specialize in obstetrics."

"What made you decide?" his friend asked.

"Well," the intern said, "when I first came to work here I was assigned to dermatology, and within a week I had developed a terrible skin rash. Next I worked in cardiology and found I was getting a heart murmur. After that I was assigned to surgery and developed appendicitis. Now that I am working in the maternity ward, I feel more relaxed."

223. An ill-tempered man went to see the doctor.

"What seems to be your trouble?" the doctor asked.

"That's what you are supposed to find out," the man said. "That's why I came to see a doctor."

"In that case," the doctor said, "I'd like you to sit in the reception room for about an hour. I want to call in a specialist. He's a veterinarian, and he is the only doctor I know who can make a medical diagnosis without asking questions."

224. The patient in the hospital seemed worried and wanted to talk to his doctor about the diagnosis.

"Are you sure it's pneumonia, doctor?" he asked. "I've heard of cases where a doctor treated a patient for pneumonia, and he ended up dying of something else."

"Don't worry," the doctor said. "When I treat a patient for pneumonia, he dies of pneumonia."

225. "Doctor," a woman said as she rushed into the office, "I want you to tell me frankly what is the matter with me."

He looked her over from head to foot, then said, "Madam, I have three things to tell you. First, you are about 50 pounds overweight. Second, your looks would be improved if you took off several layers of rouge and lipstick. And third, I'm an artist. The doctor's office is across the hall."

226. Following an automobile accident, one person was lying in the street badly injured. As a crowd began to gather, a woman rushed over to the victim and began to help him. Almost instantly, she was pushed aside by a man who said, "Please step back and let me handle everything. I've had a course in first aid."

The woman stood and watched the man work for a few minutes, and then she said to him, "When you get to the part in your first aid training where it says to call a doctor, I'm already here."

227. The hillbilly had been shot up pretty badly in a feud, and his friends had carried him to the local doctor's office.

"How bad is he hurt, Doc?" they asked.

"Well," said the doctor after a quick look at the man's wounds. "I would say that the first two wounds are fatal, but these other four aren't really very serious."

25, 194, 195, 266, 291, 377, 438, 480, 527, 530, 597, 612, 688, 693, 779, 805, 811.

DOG

228. An Eskimo's wife said to he husband, "You look terrible this morning. You must not have slept well last night."

"I didn't," he said. "I'll swear those dogs must have barked for two months last night."

229. A man was showing off his new dog—a pedigreed Pekinese.

"Where did you get him?" a friend asked.

"I had to go all the way to Peking," the man said.

"Peking?" his friend said. "Why did you go all the way to Peking? You could have found a pedigreed Pekinese right here in Cincinnati."

"Maybe so," the man said, "but who can find a parking place in Cincinnati?"

230. The family dog of questionable breed had given birth to six puppies. "That's too many animals to take care of," the father of the household said. "We've got to give the puppies away."

"Maybe we could sell them," one of the children suggested.

"That would be great," his father said. "But I doubt if anyone would buy one. We'll be lucky to give them away."

That night when the father came home from work, he was met at the door by the little boy. "Guess what," he said, "I sold one of the puppies."

"You did?" his father said. "How much did you get?"

"A hundred dollars," the boy said.

"A hundred dollars for that puppy?" the boy's father shouted. "I can't believe it. Where's the money?"

"Oh," the little boy said, "it wasn't a cash deal. I traded him for two $50 kittens."

231. A customer asked the dining room manager in a small resort hotel, "Why does your dog sit there and watch me so attentively while I eat? Does he want me to feed him?"

"No," the manager said. "It's just because you are eating off his favorite plate."

232. The doorbell rang, and the man answered it to find a friend whom he hadn't seen for some time. His friend was standing there with a large shaggy and rather muddy dog at his heels. The man invited them in, and they sat in the living room and talked about old times. The dog, after sniffing around, finally hopped on the beautiful and expensive couch and settled down for a nap, much to the host's displeasure.

Finally, the guest rose to leave. "Aren't you forgetting your dog?" asked the host.

"That's not my dog," said his friend. "I thought he was yours."

121, 205, 449.

DRESS

233. Two women were chatting about their teenage children and the various problems they faced in trying to rear them properly.

"My son has reached the stage where he runs around with his shirttail hanging out," one of the women said. "I have talked and talked to him about it, but somehow I just can't get him to tuck it in."

"Oh," said her friend, "that one was easy for me. When my boy started doing that I just sewed a bit of pink lace around the bottom of his shirts."

234. Two traveling salesmen met in a bar and began to chat and get acquainted.

"I have just made a big sale," the first man said, "and I'm trying to think of a gift to take to my wife."

"Oh," said the second man, "I know the perfect gift. Buy her a dress. No matter how many dresses she has, she'll always enjoy another one. Besides, a pretty dress will make her look beautiful. When you buy her a dress you are telling her you love her and that you want her to be beautiful and that you want her to be admired. Nothing makes a woman happier than something new to wear."

"I never thought of it that way," the first man said. "Are you a psychologist?"

"No," his new friend said. "I'm a dress manufacturer."

235. A woman waited until her husband had finished supper and was seated in front of the television set for the rest of the evening. Then she changed into a cocktail dress and paraded before him. "How do you like my new dress?" she asked. "I think it will be just the thing to wear to the cocktail party next week."

"Take it back," he said. "It's terrible. I wouldn't want to be seen at the party with you if you wore it."

"That's what I hoped you would say," she agreed. "This is my old cocktail dress. Now, I can go buy a new one. Thanks, darling."

236. Regardless of the latest style, a woman's dress should always be tight enough to show there's a woman inside but loose enough for you to know she is a lady.

190, 450, 815.

DRINKING

237. A man and his wife were driving home from a party when she said to him, "Well, you certainly did make a fool out of yourself tonight. I just hope that nobody realized you were sober."

238. The tent at the revival meeting was packed as the minister railed against every sin he could think of. After ranting 30 or 40 minutes against stealing and adultery, he finally got on the subject of drinking. At the height of his diatribe he shouted, "The evils of drink are unmeasurable. I ask you, what causes more misery in the world than drink?"

A loud voice from the rear of the tent shouted one word, "Thirst!"

239. A circus train had derailed and the car containing the lions had broken open and 10 of the animals had escaped. The sheriff quickly organized a posse to track them down. As the men were getting ready to ride off in several directions, he said, "Men, it's a bit chilly tonight, so before we go, let's go across the street to the tavern and I'll stand everybody for a few drinks."

They all gathered at the bar and ordered whiskey, except for one man. "Why aren't you drinking?" the sheriff asked. "Don't you want to get warmed up before we start out?"

"I want to stay warm all right," the man said, "but I sure don't want any whiskey before I start hunting a bunch of lions because whiskey would give me too much courage."

240. The speaker had been railing against the evils of drink. He told a horrible story about a mountaineer who had been drinking for so many years that his whole body became saturated. One night when he blew on his lamp to extinguish it, his breath ignited instead, and the poor old fellow caught fire and burned to death.

After the meeting one man shook hands with the speaker and said, "Well, sir, that story about the man burning to death sure did cure me."

"Ah," the speaker said, "you mean you have been cured of drinking tonight?"

"Not that," the man said. "You cured me of drinking near an open flame."

241. A man was driving down a country road in a drizzling rain. He came upon a man sloshing along by the side of the road with his hands in his pockets and looking miserable. The driver stopped and offered him a ride.

"Where are you going in this awful weather?" the driver asked.

"Just two miles down the road to the tavern," the man said. "I go there every day, rain or shine. Got to have my daily nip of whiskey, you know."

"I can understand that," the driver said. "But why in the world don't you keep a bottle at the house for such awful weather as we're having today?"

"That sounds like a good idea," the man said, "but at my house, whiskey don't keep."

19, 132, 134, 176, 178, 183, 204, 250, 374, 477, 575, 586.

DRIVER

242. Some people would call him a male chauvinist because he hated women drivers. Once, when he was inching his way through thick city traffic, a car driven by a curly headed blonde changed lanes in front of him so suddenly that he had to jam on his brakes in order to prevent an accident. "Look at that stupid woman driver," he shouted. "Stupid. Dumb. Stupid."

Almost at once, the car changed lanes again, and at the next stop light he pulled alongside of it. As he glanced at the blonde driver he discovered it was a young man with shoulder length hair.

"Just like I thought," the man said. "His mother probably taught him to drive."

243. The patrolman had stopped the driver for running a stop sign, changing lanes illegally, making a turn without signalling and finally parking in a restricted zone. He asked for the driver's license, and after examining it carefully said, "Yes, it looks like a genuine license all right, but tell me—how in the world did you get it?"

244. A man had just returned from an African safari with his wife. He was bragging about his trophies—several mounted heads of rather small and unimpressive animals. But the biggest trophy was the head of a huge lion. "My wife killed that one," the man said.

"Beautiful, beautiful," his friend said. "What did she kill it with, the 303 Magnum rifle you took along?"

"No," the man said. "She hit it with the four-wheel drive land-rover that we had rented."

3, 548, 738.

DRUNK

245. A man had been charged with driving while drunk and taken to court.

The judge said, "This is a serious charge. I find you guilty. And before I pass sentence I wonder if you have anything to say."

"Yes, I do, your honor," the man said. "I think it is unfair. Right there at midnight this officer stopped me and made me take that sobriety test. He didn't give me any time to study for it."

246. The town drunk was sitting on a park bench sobbing. Tears were running down his cheeks. An old friend stopped and said, "What's the matter, old fellow? You shouldn't take life so hard. What happened?"

"I did a terrible thing last week," the drunk said. "I traded my old hound dog for a bottle of whiskey and now I want him back."

"I can understand how you feel," his old friend said. "You miss his companionship and friendliness, is that it?"

"No, it's not that," the drunk said. "I'm thirsty again."

423.

ECCENTRIC

247. A young lady had announced her marriage to an older man. Even though he had made a lot of money with several inventions, some of his neighbors thought he was a bit of an oddball. Being rich, they referred to him as eccentric.

One of the young lady's friends said to her, "Why in the world do you want to marry him? Everybody knows he's half cracked."

"He may be half cracked," the young lady said, "but he sure isn't broke."

ECONOMICS

248. "A recession," explained the lecturer from the stock brokerage house, "is when your neighbor loses his job. A depression is when you lose your job. A panic is when your wife loses her job."

249. A little girl was working house to house in her neighborhood raising money for her club. When she had explained the purpose of her call to one man, he invited her into the living room and said he'd be happy to contribute.

"Take your choice," he said as he placed a one dollar bill and a dime side by side on the coffee table.

The little girl picked up the dime and said, "My mother always taught me to take the smallest piece." She then picked up the dollar bill and said, "And if you don't mind, I'll take this piece of paper to wrap it in so I'll be sure not to lose it."

43, 187, 286, 298, 454, 460, 562, 592, 632, 642.

ECONOMY

250. A world traveler was entertaining some of his friends with tales of his explorations. "There's one village on the shores of the Amazon River where you can rent a cot in a tent, get a month's supply of food, a gallon jug of whiskey and buy a wife, all for about $6.00 in American money."

One of his listeners said, "Boy, I'll bet that's lousy whiskey."

251. America is the only country in the world where men drive to lunch in $12,000 cars, wearing $20 designer neckties, order $12 steaks—and complain about hard times.

252. A woman said to her husband, "You know that new coat you bought me last week? Well, yesterday Mrs. Bergman, next door, bought one just like it."

"And now," said her husband, "I suppose you want me to buy you another new coat?"

"Well," his wife said, "it certainly would be cheaper than moving."

253. A woman was talking to her friend. "My daughter and her husband have found the perfect way to save on their food bill. They bought one of those little economy cars and they drive it over to our house every evening and have dinner with us."

254. A cheapskate does not make a pleasant person to live with, but he does make an excellent ancestor.

168, 526, 661, 808.

EDITOR

255. The editor of the local newspaper was noted for being stubborn and hardheaded.

"You always think you are right," the indignant man was saying to him. "You know good and well there have been times when you have been wrong."

"That's right," the editor said. "There was once when I was wrong."

"Aha! So you admit it," the man shouted. "When was that?"

"It happened once," the editor said, "when I thought I was wrong and I wasn't."

256. One time the city editor of a large city newspaper took a world cruise. The ship was wrecked off of the coast of Borneo, and the passengers ended up in the custody of a band of cannibals.

The next morning the shipwrecked victims were being questioned by the cannibal Chief. "What is your profession," he asked the editor.

"I am the city editor of a newspaper," he said.

"Good," the cannibal chief said. "I will promote you. Tomorrow you will be Editor-in-Chief."

257. A young lady had graduated from journalism school. She visited the office of the editor of a weekly newspaper and said, "I'm planning a career in journalism and I'd like some advice on how to run a newspaper."

"You sure did come to the wrong person," the editor said. "You should talk to some of our subscribers."

258. An irate woman stormed into the office of the local editor and shouted, "I want to see the editor."

"I'm the editor," the man wearing the green eye shade said.

"It's about that article about my daughter's coming out party!" the woman screamed.

"Do you wish to complain?" the editor asked.

"Complain?" she shouted. "Certainly not. I could have complained in a letter. I came here in person to vilify and renounce and revile someone."

598, 632, 648.

EDUCATION

259. A young lady was working to help her husband through college. Home for the Christmas vacation, her mother asked her, "Isn't it a bit embarrassing when people ask why you are working and your husband isn't?"

"Oh, no," her daughter said, "I just tell them I am working for my master's degree."

260. My son has a Ph.D.; my daughter has an A.B.; her husband has a M.A.; my nephew has a B.S.; but my husband is the only member of the family who has a J-O-B.

120, 146, 149, 434.

EGGS

261. A rather fussy housewife was shopping in the supermarket and said to the manager, "Are these eggs good?"

"Yes," he said. "These are the best eggs we have had for months."

"Do you have any that are fresher?" she asked. "I don't want any that you have had for months."

627, 681.

ELECTION

262. Two men were standing in line waiting to vote in the general election. The list of candidates was long, and the voting was slow.

One man said to his friend, "There are a lot of candidates running for each office. Why, I don't want to vote for anyone for mayor. There are eight men running, and I don't know any of them."

His friend said, "I feel the same way about the mayor's race. I don't want to vote for any of them either. And I do know them—every one."

263. Once upon a time in the deep South where everybody voted Democratic, an election was held. The County Judge had been asked to sit in the room when the votes were being tallied to act as the arbiter in case any of the votes were questionable. Things were running smoothly until one of the tally clerks said, "Hey, look at this vote. It's for the Republican candidate."

Immediately, the judge said, "Lay it aside. We'll check on it more carefully when the count is over."

Everything continued to go well until the clerks were near the end of the work. Then another one said, "Well, look here. Another Republican vote."

And that's when the judge showed his authority. "Throw both of those votes out," he said. "Some rascal has voted twice."

804.

ELEVATOR

264. A typical show-off stepped in the elevator in a Chicago skyscraper. Trying to impress the cute little operator, he said to her, "I'll bet you have your ups and downs. Don't all these stops and starts make you tired?"

"Oh," she said. "I don't mind the ups and downs and the stops and starts, but I do get sick and tired of all the jerks."

EMBEZZLEMENT

265. A man was arrested for embezzlement. He hired a lawyer and said to him, "The evidence is pretty strong against me, but I have $150,000 in cash in my safe deposit box. Do you think you can win the case?"

"I'll guarantee you one thing," the lawyer said. "You'll never go to prison with all that money."

And the lawyer was right. He didn't. He went to prison broke.

EMERGENCY

266. The frantic father called the doctor late at night. "Please hurry," he said, "my twelve year old boy just swallowed a ball point pen."

"I'll be there in about twenty minutes," the doctor said.

"What should I do until you get here?" the man wanted to know.

"Use a pencil," the doctor said.

218, 226, 301, 396, 583.

EMPLOYMENT

267. A young man was applying for a job at a large department store. The receptionist gave him a set of forms to fill in. After he had completed them, she asked him, "Do you have an account with us?"

"No, I don't," the young man said.

The receptionist then took his completed application form into the office of the personnel director and said, "There is a no-account young man waiting to see you about a job."

268. A husband who had been out of work for several weeks came in front door and cried, "Good news. I've found a great job. Good pay, only four days a week, a good health plan, good retirement, three weeks vacation every summer, and a morning and afternoon coffee break."

"Wonderful," said his wife, giving him a big hug and kiss. "When do you start work?"

"You start Monday morning," he said.

269. The office manager called in his assistant and said to him, "You know that pretty little girl, Gladys, in the typing pool?"

"Yes," the man said.

"Did you ever date her or make a pass at her?" the office manager asked.

"No, I never did," the man said.

"Did you ever write her a love letter or even call her up at night," the manager asked.

"Certainly not," the man said, "what is this questioning all about anyway?"

"Nothing," the manager said, "except that we wanted to be sure to find just the right man for a delicate job. And you are the man. We want you to fire her."

270. A man was looking for a job. In answer to the question, "Why did you leave your last place of employment?" he wrote in the word "Turnover."

The personnel director questioned him. "What did you mean by turnover?" he asked.

"They turned my job over to somebody else," the man said.

271. A woman was urging her husband to hire a lazy nephew. "He needs a job," she said. "You have hundreds of workers at the plant and I'm sure you can find something for him to do."

"We don't have an opening," her husband said. "Business is slow at the moment and we really don't have enough work to keep our present employees busy."

"That's all right," the man's wife said. "The little work he would do wouldn't even be noticed anyway."

22, 503.

ENGAGEMENT

272. Two young ladies ran into each other for the first time in weeks while they were shopping. "Oh, it's good to see you," the first one said. "I haven't seen you since your engagement party. Have you set the date for the wedding?"

"The wedding's off," her friend said. "Charlie and I have broken up."

"What happened?" the first one said.

"Nothing special," her friend said. "I found that my love for him became weaker and weaker and finally disappeared altogether."

"That's too bad," the first one said. "Did you return his ring?"

"Oh, no," her friend said. "My love for the ring is just as strong as ever."

ENTHUSIASM

273. A young man who had graduated from college with a degree in business administration decided to go into business for himself. After much careful study he settled on the idea of opening a neighborhood convenience store. He called on the banker and asked him for a $50,000 loan.

"That's an awful lot of money for a young man," the banker said. "Can you give me a statement?"

"Certainly," the young businessman said. "I'm enthusiastic."

534.

EVIDENCE

274. The local newspaper received an invitation for an annual dance from a nearby nudist colony. Thinking it might be interesting, the editor sent one of his cub reporters.

When the reporter returned to the newspaper, the editor asked him how things went. "It was an exciting affair. Nobody had any clothes on. Even the butler who opened the door was naked."

'If he was naked," the editor asked, "how did you know it was the butler?"

"Well," the reporter said, "it certainly wasn't the maid."

192, 445.

EXERCISE

275. A man who lived in Cincinnati went to his doctor for a complete checkup. "You need to exercise," the doctor told him. "I want you to run every day to build yourself up. Start with one mile the first day; increase it a mile a day until you are running ten miles a day."

"Sundays too?" the man asked.

"Ten miles a day, seven days a week,"the doctor told him. "And give me a call in three weeks."

Three weeks later the man called the doctor and said, "I feel a lot better."

"Fine," the doctor said. "I'd like to check you over again. How about dropping by my office at 2:30 this afternoon?"

"This afternoon?" the man cried. "I can't. I've been running like you said, and I'm in Zanesville."

21.

EXHIBITION

276. A lovely young girl with a beautiful figure said to the manager of the ladies' dress shop, "May I try on that bikini in the window?"

"It's all right with me if you want to do it," he said "Business has been rather slow this morning and it might help draw a crowd."

EXPERIENCE

277. Several weeks after a young man had been hired, he was called into the office of the personnel director. "What is the meaning of this?" the director asked. "When you applied for the job you told us you had five years experience. Now we discover this is the first job you ever held."

"Well," the young man said, "in your advertisement you said you wanted somebody with imagination."

278. A man was making his weekly check with the unemployment office. "I think we have a job for you this week," the manager said. "There is an opening at the Eagle Laundry. Would you like to apply for it?"

"I need a job real bad," the man said, "but I don't think they would hire me. You see, I've never washed an eagle."

280, 506, 673, 707, 828.

EXPERT

279. The woman who mopped the floors at night in the big office building was bragging to her long-time friend.

"You should have seen those floors when I went to work there," she said. "They were awful. You couldn't tell what color they were supposed to be. Now I've got them polished and waxed to where you can see your reflection in them. Why only last week two ladies and the mailman slipped and fell."

EXTRAVAGANCE

280. The 10 year old boy was visiting his grandparents for the first time in five or six years. They were so proud of his neat appearance and his good manners that they took him to the theatre and after that to a swanky restaurant.

"This is a fancy restaurant," they told him. "You can have anything you want to eat. Why don't you order something you never had before?"

After looking over the menu, the young fellow ordered a deluxe hamburger.

"A hamburger?" his grandmother said. "You eat them at home all the time. Like we said, why don't you order something you never had before?"

"That's what I did," the boy said. "This will be the first time I ever ate a $3.95 hamburger."

FAMILIAR

281. Two men were seated at a bar. One was staring at the other with an intense gaze. The other one finally said, "You have been staring at me for half an hour. Is there something the matter?"

"No," the first fellow said, "except that you remind me of my girlfriend. If it weren't for the mustache you would look exactly like her. You could be her twin."

"Mustache?" the man said. "But I don't have a mustache."

"I know," the first man said, "but she does."

FARMER

282. A young man and his girlfriend were walking down a country lane. On the other side of a fence was a field of colorful wild flowers. The young man climbed the fence to pick a bouquet for his girlfriend. Suddenly he saw a bull staring at him from a distance of about 20 feet. A little frightened, he called to a farmer who was standing in the next field, "Hey, is this bull safe?"

"Well," said the farmer, "I'm sure he's a lot safer than you are at this moment."

283. A man who had borrowed rather heavily on his orange grove went to see his banker. "I can't meet my note for $8,000 that falls due next Wednesday because of the big freeze we had last winter. You'll have to give me an extension."

"I can't give you an extension," the banker said. "The freeze hit everyone and you'll have to pay off your note on Wednesday."

"I don't think you understand the problem," the citrus grower said. "Were you ever in the citrus business?"

"No," said the banker.

"Well," said the man, "starting next Wednesday, you will be."

284. A farmer married a school teacher and from the very first day she was continually correcting his English.

One evening shortly after they were married, a car came in their driveway. "Hey," the farmer said to his wife, "that will be Bill Wilson. You'll enjoy meeting him, he always has some exciting tales to tell."

"You shouldn't call him Bill," his wife said. "You should call him William. And never say tale, you should say anecdote."

After his friend had left that evening, the farmer said, "Well, I guess it's time to put out the lights and go to bed."

"Don't say put out," his wife reminded him. "Say extinguish."

During the middle of the night they were awakened by a noise downstairs. The farmer rushed down to investigate. In a few minutes everything was quiet, and when he returned to bed his wife asked him what the noise was all about.

"Nothing much," he said. "An old William-goat had just wandered up on the back porch. I took care of him all right. I grabbed him by his anecdote and extinguished him."

285. The farmer was showing the county agent his problem. "Everything is dry," he said. "For a while I was able to get some water from the creek, but finally it dried up too."

"When you saw that the creek was going dry, why didn't you dam it?" the county agent asked.

"Oh, I did," the man said, "and I called it a lot of other names too, but profanity didn't seem to help."

286. A farmer from Southern Illinois was visiting a friend in Chicago. They had a sandwich for lunch at one of Chicago's fanciest restaurants. As they paid their check, the farmer said, "According to what they charged for that ham sandwich, I've got a hog back on my farm that's worth about $6,500."

287. A farmer was visiting with his friend over the fence on the lower forty. "I just installed something at the house that the grandchildren are getting a real bang out of."

"What's that?" asked the other farmer, "one of those color television sets?"

"No," said his friend, "a screen door."

288. The big executive from the city was looking at a farm as a place to retire. The real estate man was showing him one of the most beautiful farms in the State. It was on a small hill, and the farmhouse overlooked more than 400 acres.

"I don't like it," the city man said. "Let's look at something else."

"Okay," the real estate man said, "but to help me find you something that you will like, tell me what is wrong with this farm. What is it that you don't like?"

"For one thing," the city man said, "you can see the whole farm from the house. There isn't any place where I can hide from my wife."

289. The farmer was a chronic complainer. For years, he complained, the weather had been against him, the bugs had eaten up what little produce he could grow, and always the market was low when something was ready to sell. Then came the year when he hit it big. No bugs, perfect weather, a huge crop and high prices.

"Well, you finally made it big," a friend said.

"Fair, just fair," the farmer said. "Besides, a harvest like this is pretty hard on the soil."

290. A man drove into the farmer's yard and asked him, "How much is that old bull of yours worth?"

The farmer thought for a moment and said, "Are you the tax assessor, or do you want to buy him, or has he been run over by a truck?"

291. Just a few days after the young doctor had opened his office in a small community, he was awakened at 4:30 in the morning by someone ringing his doorbell. Throwing on a robe and rushing to the door to take care of what he knew must be a terrible emergency, he found a farmer dressed in overalls standing there.

"What's the emergency?" the doctor cried.

"Emergency? There's no emergency," the farmer said. "You told me to come for a blood test before I had eaten breakfast and here I am."

292. The farmer and his wife were entertaining friends from the city. As a special treat she was serving four year old ham, a delicacy she was sure her guests had never eaten.

"I hope you enjoy the ham," she said. "Jeff cured it himself."

"Cured it?" her guest asked as he dropped his fork. "What sort of disease did it have?"

172, 568, 605, 751.

FASHION

293. A woman took her seat in the theater in front of a man and his wife. She was wearing a rather large hat and, thinking it might obstruct the view of the couple behind her, she turned and said to the man, "Excuse me, does my hat bother you?"

"No," he said. "It doesn't bother me, but it's about to kill my wife. She bought one yesterday just like it."

236, 252.

FATHER

294. Two men were having lunch when one of them nodded his head in the direction of another table and said, "Look at old Don having lunch with that pretty young girl. I wonder who she is."

"Oh," said his friend, "that's a distant relative of his. It's his teenage daughter."

528.

FIGHT

295. A woman heard a commotion in her back yard and rushed out to find her little girl in a knock-down-drag-out fight with the little boy next door.

She separated them quickly and said to her little girl, "You shouldn't hit your friend."

"But," the little girl cried, "he hit me first."

"That doesn't matter," her mother said. "Remember you are a little lady. You are supposed to outtalk him."

296. A sudden screaming and crying erupted from the recreation room. Mother rushed in to find her two little ones fighting tooth and nail. "Stop it!" she cried.

Once she had them quiet, she said, "Now, who started the trouble this time?"

"She did," the oldest one said. "She started it when she hit me back."

424.

FINANCE

297. Two men were chatting about their children who were away at school. "What does your son plan to do when he finishes college?" the first man asked.

"I don't think he's decided yet," his friend said, "but judging from his letters to us, he would make an excellent professional fund-raiser."

298. A young married couple were applying for a short-time loan. "How much money do you need and what is the purpose of the loan?" the banker asked.

"Oh," said the bride before her husband could answer, "we just need enough money to tide us over until we can get some credit cards."

43, 181, 637.

FIRE DEPARTMENT

299. A retired businessman from the North moved to a small town in Florida. As soon as he was settled in his new home, the local people invited him to join such things as shuffle board clubs and bridge clubs and craft clubs. One day, a group visited his home and invited him to become a member of the local volunteer fire department.

"I like that," he said. "I was a member of my volunteer fire department back home. But I'm not as young as I used to be, and I'm afraid I might not be much help. That going up and down ladders will be a bit more than I might be able to take."

"Oh, don't worry about that," the local chief said. "Mostly by the time we get to the fire, there isn't anything to lean the ladder up against anyway."

FIREMAN

300. The local fire chief had worked out an orderly plan for a speedy evacuation of the local grammar school in case of fire. After several practice fire drills, the chief told the principal, "One more time. This is it. This time we'll hold a stop watch on the kids to see how well they do."

Bells rang, kids lined up and marched according to the chief's plan, and nobody made a mistake or lost a moment's time. Perfect. No confusion. The school house was empty.

Time: three minutes, sixteen seconds.

Fifteen minutes later it was time for recess. The bells rang. The kids scrambled. And soon the school house was again empty.

Time: two minutes, three seconds.

136.

FIRST AID

301. A young housewife was telling her husband about the events of the day as they were having dinner.

"A terrible thing happened at the shopping mall," she said. "As I was coming out of the supermarket with my groceries, a man who was repairing their huge electric sign slipped and fell off of his ladder. He landed about three feet from me and the sign fell on top of him. There was broken glass everywhere. You never saw so much blood in all your life."

"What did you do?" her husband asked.

"Oh, I didn't lose my head," she said. "Remember that first aid course I took last year? It sure came in handy. I knew exactly what to do. I immediately sat on the curb and put my head between my knees. And it worked. I didn't faint."

302. A hunter was buying a survival kit at the sporting goods store and the salesman was showing him what was in the kit and how to use each item. He had explained about the flint and steel for making a fire, the plastic poncho to keep him warm and half a dozen other items. Then he said, "And this is your little bottle of gin and vermouth to expedite your rescue."

"What do you mean, expedite my rescue?" the hunter said.

"Well," the salesman said, "as everyone who has ever mixed a martini knows, as soon as you start to mix a martini, people will suddenly appear from everywhere to tell you how to do it."

266.

FISHING

303. A fishing pole is a long stick with a hook and line at one end and a liar at the other.

304. A woman had just returned from a fishing trip with her husband and was telling a friend about it. "It was terrible," she said. "I did everything wrong. I scraped the bottom of the boat with my feet and scared the fish away; I used the wrong kind of bait; I didn't cast far enough; I didn't set the hook properly; I talked too loud—and besides, I caught more fish than he did."

305. The only time I ever heard a fisherman tell the truth was when he called his fishing buddy a liar.

306. Two men were planning to go fishing. "I'll bring the boat and motor," the first man said, "and you bring the lunch."

Early the next morning the first man drove up to the second man's house with his boat and motor and honked his horn. His friend was ready and as he got in the car he put the lunch in the back seat.

"What did you bring for lunch?" the first man asked.

"Four six-packs of beer and half a dozen buttered biscuits," his friend said.

"What in the world do you expect to do with all those biscuits?" the first man asked.

307. A little fellow who was fishing off the end of a pier lost his balance while trying to land a fish and fell in the lake.

Several men who also were fishing nearby rushed to his aid and pulled him out.

"How did you come to fall in?" one of the men asked him.

"I didn't come to fall in," the kid said. "I came to fish."

308. A man was berating a farmer friend of his for not working harder. "You've got a good spread of land and you could make a lot of money if you would spend more time farming and less time fishing."

"Take a look at this map of the world," the farmer said. "You will notice that two-thirds of the earth is water and one third is land. So it seems to me that man is supposed to fish two-thirds of the time and farm one-third."

FLOOD

309. A grandmother from the Bayou country of Louisiana was visiting her well-to-do grandson in New Orleans. This was her first visit to the city, and her grandson was showing her his penthouse apartment on top of a downtown hotel.

As his grandmother looked out over the city and the great Mississippi River sweeping past, she said, "One thing for sure. Living here you don't have any worries when the river rises."

FLOWERS

310. A man visited a florist's shop and asked for an eight inch high red geranium.

"I'm sorry we don't have any geraniums in stock at the moment," the florist said. "But we have some lovely African violets. How about a few of those?"

"No, not this time," the man said. "You see, my wife is coming home tomorrow, and it was a potted red geranium, about eight inches tall that I was supposed to water while she was away."

784.

FOOD

311. A professor of botany at the local college had a delightful hobby. Every weekend he would tramp through the woods gathering mushrooms. On many occasions he would come home with more mushrooms than his own family could use; so he would give some to his neighbors.

One day he stopped a neighbor and said, "How did you like the mushrooms I gave you last week?"

"Oh," the woman said, "They were absolutely delicious. My aunt and uncle were over and they said they had never tasted more flavorful mushrooms. We sure thank you for being so generous and thinking of us."

"I'm glad everyone enjoyed them," the botanist said. "Some people are allergic to mushrooms. No one had any side effects or got the least bit sick from them, did they?"

"Oh, no," the woman said. "Like I told you, they were the most delicious mushrooms you have ever given us."

"Hooray!" the botanist shouted. "I have just discovered a new species of non-poisonous mushrooms."

312. The bride's first dinner was over, and as she cleared the dishes from the table, she said to her husband, "What will I get, darling, if I cook a dinner like that for you from now on?"

"Sooner or later," he said, "you'll get my life insurance."

313. A man was dining out with his wife, and they went to an Italian restaurant. As they were looking over the menu, the man said to his wife, "How do you pronounce that Italian dish that I'm so wild about?"

Without looking up from the menu, his wife said, "Gina Lollobrigida."

314. The little lady was celebrating her 85th birthday. Among her visitors was a granddaughter who said to her, "Ever since I can remember, I've thought of you as a busy person. You have always been a great worker in the church; you have raised a large family; you have always been ready to help anyone who is sick; and through it all you seem to be relaxed and happy and contented. What has given you so much energy and peace of mind? What has kept you so full of life all these years?"

Never had the granddaughter seen a look of greater contentment as the lady whispered one word, "Food."

104, 196, 231, 292, 306, 466, 619, 620.

FOOTBALL

315. An American was entertaining a friend from England. He took him to see the Superbowl game. The Englishman followed the action with great interest and seemed especially interested in watching each team go into a huddle before every play.

When the game was over, the American asked his friend, "Well, what do you think of American football? How did you like the game?"

"I think it's a great sport," the Englishman said, "but I do think the chaps could do better if they didn't hold so many committee meetings."

316. The man was watching the football game on TV. Finally, he began to shout at nobody in particular, "Look at

that halfback. He's fumbled three times and every time the other team has recovered and scored. Why don't they take the stupid jerk out of the game?"

His little eight year old boy said, "Maybe it's his ball."

317. Week after week the woman's husband would watch the football game on television while she did housework. One day, while he was watching the game and she was washing the ceiling, she boiled over and shouted at him, "Hey, you! If I should fall off this step-ladder would you mind calling an ambulance during half-time?"

318. The football referee had penalized the offensive team 15 yards for unnecessary roughness. After he had paced off the yardage and was placing the ball in position, the man who had committed the foul screamed at him, "You're the worst referee I ever saw. I think you stink."

The referee quietly stood up and paced off another 15 yard penalty. He then turned to the angry player and said, "How do I smell from here?"

319. The man had been glued to the televison set through three football games when his wife said to him with a tear in her voice, "You don't love me like you used to. I do believe you love football more than you do me."

"Maybe," he said, "but I love you more than basketball and hockey put together."

320. "How are you getting along with your new girlfriend?" a fellow asked a football star.

"Not so good," he said. "She told me last night that she would be faithful to the end."

"Why, man, that's great," the first fellow said. "What's wrong with that?"

"Because," his friend said, "I'm the quarterback."

321. A husband came home from work and found his wife sobbing in front of the television set. "How in the world can you get worked up over the troubles of people in those soap operas day after day?" he asked.

"I suppose it's the same as you screaming and getting excited when you see men you don't even know grab a little ball and chase up and down the field with it."

322. The football addict had fallen asleep in his chair while watching a football game on television. His wife went to bed thinking that he would eventually wake up and follow her. Instead, he was still there, sound asleep, the next morning. Knowing he had to get to work she shook him awake and said, "Wake up, it's twenty to seven."

He opened his eyes slowly and asked sleepily, "In whose favor?"

378, 528.

FORGIVENESS

323. A man had too much to drink at a party. First, he made a foolish spectacle of himself, then he passed out. Friends had to help his wife take him home and put him to bed. He was very remorseful and asked his wife to forgive him. She said she understood and that she would forgive and forget. However, as the months went by, she would refer to the incident from time to time. After a while he became tired of hearing about it. "I thought you said you were going to forgive and forget," he said.

"I have forgiven and forgotten," she said, "but I just don't want you to forget that I have forgiven and forgotten."

FORTUNE TELLER

324. "Cross my palm with 20 dollars," said the fortune teller, "and I'll answer your questions."

The man gave the fortune teller 20 dollars and she said, "You now have two questions that I'll guarantee to answer."

"Isn't 20 dollars a pretty high price to pay for just two questions?" the man asked.

"Yes, it is," the fortune teller said. "Now what is your second question?"

FREEDOM

325. "This is a free country," the speaker said. "In America a man can stand up and speak the truth; that is, if he isn't afraid of his wife or his mother-in-law or the neighbors or his boss, and if he thinks it won't hurt his reputation or his business—and if he is sure the Internal Revenue Service is not listening."

FRIENDSHIP

326. Two members of a luncheon club were sitting next to each other at the weekly meeting.

"Would you do me a favor," the first one asked. "How about lending me $100 until the first of the month?"

"I would except for one thing," the other man said. "You know the old saying, 'Lend a dollar, lose a friend.' So, I make it a point never to lend money to my friends."

"I think you are right," the first man said, "but, let's face it, we really aren't very good friends to begin with."

327. A man was moving slowly with a tightly-packed crowd at a ball game when he thought he recognized a friend just ahead. Giving the man a mighty slap on the back, he said, "Hi, Elmer. Long time, no see. How are things?"

Imagine his embarrassment when he discovered that the man was a complete stranger. "I'm so sorry," he said. "I thought you were a friend of mine, good old Elmer. Please excuse me."

"I'll excuse you," said the man, "but suppose I was Elmer. Why did you have to hit him so hard?"

328. "Poor old Joe," a man said to his friend, "since he lost all of his money, half of his friends have deserted him."

"What about the other half?" his friend asked.

"They don't know he's broke," the first man said.

329. Two men were chatting when the name of a mutual friend was mentioned. "Are you a friend of Harry's?" the first man asked.

"Are we friends?" the other man said. "We grew up together in this town. I've known him since the third grade. There's nothing I wouldn't do for Harry and there's nothing he wouldn't do for me. In fact, for 40 years, as I said, we've gone through life together, doing absolutely nothing for each other."

FRIGHT

330. Two men were chatting. "Did you hear about the terrible fright Bob got on his wedding day?"

"Yes," his friend said. "I was at the wedding. I saw her."

FUNERAL DIRECTOR

331. The vice-president of a company died, and bright and early the next morning an ambitious junior officer of the company came to see the president and said, "It certainly is sad about the tragedy, but I am sure you feel that everything should keep going. I don't want to seem presumptuous, but I would like to talk to you about me taking his place."

His boss never hesitated a minute. "That's fine with me if you can work it out with the funeral director."

FUTURE

332. "I don't guess I'll ever get married," a young fellow said to his friend.

"Why not?"

"Well, my girlfriend won't marry me when I'm drunk and I'm sure not going to marry her when I'm sober."

333. Two strangers met in a bar and were chatting. "It's a sad world," the first man said as he looked ready to cry in his beer.

"What's so sad about it?" his new friend said. "Why do you look so worried?"

"It's my future," the other fellow said, "my hopeless future."

"Why is your future so hopeless?"

"My past," he said.

334. "My biggest criticism of Tom," a fellow told his friend, "is that he doesn't think and plan ahead."

"What do you mean?" his friend asked.

"Well, he's getting married next month," the first fellow said, "and he hasn't even tried to find a job for his wife."

377.

GAMBLER

335. Two fellows sitting at a bar were talking about a friend. "I can't understand why Jeff loses so much money at the race track," the first man said, "and yet is so lucky whenever he plays poker."

"That's easy to understand," his friend said. "They never let him shuffle the horses at the track."

336. A man and his bride visited Las Vegas on their honeymoon. This was the first time the woman had ever been near a gambling casino, and her excitement knew no bounds. "Let's play roulette," she said.

So her husband gave her a $5.00 chip.

"What number should I play?" she asked him.

"Why don't you play your age," he said.

So, she placed the bet on number 26. The wheel turned, and the little ball rolled round and round. Finally, it settled in number 34.

And the bride fainted.

337. "Hey, Joe," a fellow shouted to his friend, "I hear you hit big yesterday on the numbers. Congratulations."

"Yes," Joe said, "I guess 43 is my lucky number."

'Man, that was a good number. How did you pick 43?"

"I had a dream," the lucky man said. "I saw a man unloading a boat with seven fish. Then I saw a woman carrying seven loaves of bread under her arm. Then I saw seven cars parked in front of the post office. While I was standing there, seven kids ran across the street and seven other kids came by riding their bicycles. That made six times I saw seven in my dream. So, six times seven—and I bet on 43."

"You're stupid," the first man said. "Six times seven is 42, and you bet on number 43."

"Look," said the gambler, "you be the mathematician. I'll bet the numbers."

338. A confirmed horse player hadn't been in church in years even though his wife attended every Sunday. One Easter, with a bit of nagging and persuasion, he went to church with her.

On the way home, he said to her, "It wasn't bad. The church was airconditioned, the pews were cushioned and the singing was great. Did you notice people looking at me when I joined in with my deep baritone voice?"

"Yes, I noticed," his wife said. "But when we go next time, and you sing, be sure you sing Hallelujah, Hallelujah and not Hialeah, Hialeah."

339. A man took his talking dog to a bar on Lincoln's birthday and began to brag about his ability to remember facts about history. Before getting his dog to perform, the man picked up a few bets from the spectators. "Now, tell us," he said to his dog when he was ready, "what day was Lincoln born?" The dog never said a word.

Again, the man urged his dog to talk. He asked him a dozen questions about the great president and got nothing but silence. In disgust he finally paid off his bets and left the bar.

As he drove away he said to his dog, "Why didn't you say anything? You cost me 20 dollars."

"Sure," said the dog. "But get smart when you show me off. Think of the odds you'll get when you go back a few days from now on George Washington's birthday."

389, 584, 730.

GAMES

340. The cocktail party was in full swing, with everybody chatting and getting acquainted. One man, with obvious wolfish intent, singled out a beautiful girl who appeared to be alone. "Well, well," he said, "the party was nothing but dull until this moment. Now that I have met the prettiest girl here, the party will liven up. You and I could have a lot of fun playing games together."

"What did you have in mind?" she asked.

"What about Post Office?" he said. "That's a good way to get acquainted."

"Post Office?" she said. "That's just a kid's game. Too old fashioned. I have a better idea. Why don't we play Building and Loan?"

"That sounds all right with me," he said. "How do you play Building and Loan?"

"That's easy," she said. "You just get out of the building and leave me alone."

GENEALOGY

341. A man visited a professional genealogist and asked how much it would cost to have his family tree traced. "That depends on how far back you want it traced and how difficult it is to search the records. It might cost several hundred dollars or several thousand."

"That sounds expensive," the man said. "Isn't there an easier way to do it?"

"Oh," said the genealogist, "the easiest way to have your family tree researched is for you to run for public office."

GENEROSITY

342. The volunteer worker for the United Givers Drive called on the town's leading banker. Thinking he would flatter him into making a sizable contribution, he said, "I'm honored that your name was on my list because you are rumored to be the most generous man in town."

The banker quietly wrote out a check and handed it to the man and said, "Here's a check for $10.00. Now you can start denying that rumor."

126.

GIFT

343. A young lady was admiring the diamond engagement ring her boyfriend had given her several months before. "Every time I look at it I think of you," she said. "It's beautiful. And I understand there isn't anything in the world as hard as a diamond, is that right?"

"Yes, one thing is harder," he said. "And that's making the monthly payments on one."

344. A man wanted to be nice to his wife on their 10th wedding anniversary. "You can have a choice," he said. "Either a mink coat or a trip to Paris."

"Oh, how exciting," she said. "Let's take the trip to Paris—because I understand that we can find real bargains in mink coats over there."

345. "Why are you so unhappy with the birthday present Uncle George sent you?" a woman asked her son. "I remember him asking you whether you wanted a small check or a large check."

"Yes," said her son, "but I didn't know he was talking about a necktie."

346. The college boy received a sports car from his parents when he graduated. On the steering wheel was this note: "Best wishes from Mama and Pauper."

87, 88, 103, 106, 139, 140, 147, 420, 584, 629, 682.

GOLF

347. A man and his wife were having Sunday breakfast on their patio. "My, what a beautiful day," she said. "This is perfect weather, and I think it would be fun if we went somewhere together. And I mean it, too. This is one day that you aren't going to sneak off and play golf with your buddies."

"Why, honey," he said. "Golf is the farthest thing from my mind. Will you please pass me the bread and putter?"

348. Two men were chatting and getting acquainted in the recreation hall of a mobile home park in Florida.

"It's good to be in Florida for the winter," the first man said. "Tomorrow I'll be out playing golf. I play nearly every day while I'm here. Of course, you play golf?"

The second man felt a bit intimidated when the first man said "of course," and since he didn't want to seem out of things, he lied and said, "Yes, I play nearly every day myself."

"Then you must be pretty good," the first man said. "I play in the low seventies myself."

"So do I," the non-golfer said, "but if it gets any colder than that, I come back to the trailer and watch television."

349. A bystander, watching a golf match, was struck in the head by a ball. With a knot on his head and fury in his heart, he picked up the ball and rushed toward the player who had hit him. "You nearly killed me!" he shouted. "I'm going to sue you. I'm going to sue you for $5,000. That's what I'm going to do."

"But," said the golfer, "I cried fore."

"I think that's letting you off mighty easy," the injured man said, "but for a quick settlement, I'll take it."

350. Time after time the duffer would hit his brand new balls where they couldn't be found: into the lake, out of bounds across the highway, into the deep woods, and even one into a storm sewer that was under construction near the golf course.

Finally, one of the members of his foursome said, "Why in the world don't you use an old ball on those difficult shots?"

"An old ball?" asked the duffer. "Can't you tell from the way I play that I never had an old ball?"

351. A man was browsing through the used books at the annual library clearance sale and bought a copy of Hemingway's *Across the River and into the Trees.* He thought it was a book about golf.

352. Two hard of hearing friends pulled up side by side in their convertibles at a stop light. Each had his golf bag on the back seat in plain sight.

"You going to the club for a round of golf?" the first man asked.

"No," the second man shouted back, "I'm going to the club for a round of golf."

"Oh," shouted the first fellow. "I thought maybe you were going out to the club for a round of golf."

353. A man had just oiled the lawn mower for his wife before leaving for the country club to play golf. As he was backing the car out of the driveway, she came screaming out of the house.

"Golf, golf, golf!" she shouted. "That's all you think about. While I am here mowing the lawn you're out playing golf. One of these days when you come home you'll find that I've had enough. I won't be here. I'll be packed up and moved out—forever."

"Now, now, honey," he said in a soft and soothing voice. "You shouldn't talk like that. You know very well you can't bribe me with promises."

354. The golfer was having a disastrous day. He had bogeyed nine holes and double bogeyed three. Then, on the 18th hole he was two feet from the pin for a possible birdie. But, even then, he couldn't do it. He took three strokes to sink his ball for another bogey.

At that point, understandably, his nerves cracked and he went to pieces. He threw his ball into the woods, broke his putter over his knee and sat on the green and began to weep. "Oh!" he moaned. "Oh! Oh! I'm going to give it up. I'm going to give it up. I'm going to give it up."

Another golfer who was standing nearby said, "Don't take it so hard. Just because of a bad day, don't give up golf."

"Oh, no," the man moaned, "I'm not going to give up golf. I'm going to give up the ministry."

355. One golfer had just blasted out of a sand trap, and his ball was lying about two feet from the hole. Another member of the foursome whose ball was lying about 20 feet from the hole, was now preparing to putt. The first golfer said, "The traps on this course sure are annoying, aren't they?"

The golfer who was putting said, "They sure are. How about shutting yours?"

356. The man had made a hole-in-one, and as so often happens, it became his chief topic of conversation. After several weeks of listening to him tell about it, his wife began to weary of the story. Then, one night when he was telling dinner guests about it, one of them said, "I think that's wonderful. Man, that's a thrill of a lifetime."

"Yes," his wife said. "It's too bad he can't have it stuffed."

209.

GOOD OLD DAYS

357. A mother was telling her little girl about life on the farm when she was growing up. "We had lots of fun down on the farm," she said. "I had a swing made out of an old automobile tire that swung from an oak tree, and I had a pony to ride, and I used to slide down the haystack in the summer and ride the sleigh in winter."

Her daughter was all eyes as she said, "I sure do wish I had met you sooner."

657.

GOSSIP

358. One thing you have to say about Alice," a woman said to her friend. "She never repeats gossip. If you don't hear her the first time, you've missed it."

359. One woman to another: "I make it a point never to say anything about a person unless it is good. Now, let me tell you about Gladys—and is this good!"

532, 800.

GOVERNMENT

360. The senior citizen took his government check to the bank to cash it. Although it was plainly marked, "Do not fold, staple, spindle or mutilate," the old man had rumpled it and folded it.

When he endorsed it the teller said, "You should be more careful with your checks. You shouldn't rumple them or fold them. The government doesn't like that."

"Well," the senior citizen said, "maybe that helps make us even, because there are a few things that the government does that I don't like."

GOVERNOR

361. The governor of the state had just addressed a huge crowd gathered for the annual Labor Day picnic in a county seat town.

One of his admirers said, "You must get a great thrill to know this crowd of people came out to hear you speak."

"Yes," the governor said. "You are right. I do get a great thrill over seeing such a large crowd. But as I stand there and look at them, I also think how much larger it would be if I were being hanged."

GRADUATION

362. The women at the bridge club were bragging about their children. One woman said that her daughter was valedictorian of her class. Another one explained that her son was third in his class and has won a four year scholarship to a big university. "And how did your daughter do?" they asked the woman who had kept quiet through the entire conversation.

"Oh, she did fine," the woman said. "She graduated in the top 70% of her class."

363. A university alumnus had returned to his alma mater for the graduation exercises. Later he was chatting with the president and said, "I noted that you awarded half a dozen honorary degrees, and all of them were given to wealthy people. Isn't that a bit obvious? Aren't you doing that just to get them to give money to the school?"

"Not exactly," the university president said, "but I will admit that most of our new buildings are being paid for by degrees."

663.

GRAMMAR

364. The second grade teacher had sent the children to the board to work arithmetic problems. One little fellow said, "I ain't got no chalk."

"That isn't right," the teacher said. "The right way to say it is, 'I don't have any chalk; you don't have any chalk; we don't have any chalk; they don't have any chalk.' Now, do you understand?"

"No," said the little boy, "what happened to all the chalk?"

162, 284.

GRANDFATHER

365. Grandfather was visiting his son and his family for the first time in two years. His little three year old granddaughter, Denise, was fascinated with her grandfather. She was especially intrigued with his false teeth and his hair piece. She stared with rapt attention as he removed them.

"Do that again, Grandaddy," she said. "That's funny."

Her obliging grandfather removed his teeth and then popped them back in his mouth. He removed his hair piece and waved it around and replaced it to cover his bald spot. "Now what do you want me to do?" he asked Denise.

"Now," she said eagerly, "let me see you take off your ears."

23.

GRANDMOTHER

366. A mother told her next door neighbor, "I don't know what to do about little Alice. The only way I can make her behave is to threaten to take away her grandmother."

367. A little boy wrote this letter to his grandmother, "Dear Grandmother, I'm very sorry that I forgot your birthday last week. It would serve me right if you forgot mine next Tuesday."

368. Grandmother was walking her daughter's children in the park when a lady said to her. "My what charming children. How old are they?"

"The doctor is five," the proud grandmother said, "and the ambassador is three."

369. The wedding date had been set, and the groom-to-be was seeking advice from a married friend of his. "What should I call my mother-in-law?" he asked. "I won't feel comfortable calling her 'Mother' because that's what I call my own mother. And if I call her 'Mrs. Wilson,' that wouldn't sound right either. How did you solve the problem?"

"Nothing to it," his wise friend said. "For the first nine months you just say 'Hey.' After that you can call her 'Grandma.' "

370. The little boy's grandmother was visiting for the first time since he was a tiny baby, and of course he did not remember ever having seen her.

In the excitement of her arrival she picked up the little fellow and said, "My, what a fine looking young man."

He looked at her and said, "I don't know you. What's your name?"

"I'm your grandmother," she said. "I'm your grandmother on your father's side."

"Well," the little boy said, "you won't be here very long until you find out you're on the wrong side."

29, 82, 102, 453, 454.

GRIEF

371. A woman was almost panic-stricken as she called her long-time friend on the telephone.

"Oh, dear," she said, "I just have to talk to someone. I just found this note on my kitchen table. My husband has run off with another woman. Gone. Gone. Gone forever. I'm so full of pent-up emotion I don't know what to do. I'm sure that any minute I'll just let go."

"That's the thing to do," her friend said. "Just give in to emotions. Let yourself go. Nothing will do you any more good right now than a good laugh."

HAIRCUT

372. The long-haired young man finally had his shoulder length tresses cut off. As he emerged from the barber shop with his short military type trim, one of his buddies said, "Hey, man, you don't look like the same person." Then trying to be funny, he said, "How much weight did you lose?"

"A hundred and eighty-five pounds," the fellow said. "I got my dad off my back."

71.

HALLOWEEN

373. The door bell rang on Halloween and the man went to the door with a few goodies to hand out. When he opened the door, there, holding an open bag, stood a little three year old girl dressed like an old witch. In spite of her horrible costume, the little girl was bare faced.

"Here is some candy," the man said as he dropped it in her bag. "But why aren't you wearing your witch's mask?"

She looked up at him with her big eyes and said shyly, "Because I'm afraid of it."

HANGOVER

374. A woman was chatting with a friend on the phone. "Jim's still in bed. He's suffering from a hangover this morning."

"Oh," her friend said, "did you go to a wild party last night?"

"No," the woman said. "He was on the late champagne flight that was coming in from San Francisco last night, and the plane was stuck in a holding pattern over the airport here for two hours."

HEALTH

375. Two women were chatting in a beauty parlor. The first was telling her friend all about her ailments. "I've got a bad case of arthritis," she said, "and my ankle is sprained. I am short of breath, I can hardly swallow, and besides that there is a buzzing in my ears."

"My goodness," her friend said. "You sure must be healthy to be able to stand all that pain."

376. A tourist visited an Indian trading post on an Indian reservation in New Mexico. Among the many souvenirs she bought was a beautiful peace pipe with an intricate design which included some strange Indian writing.

Excited over her purchase, she sough out an Indian and asked him to translate the writings.

"Very easy," the Indian said. "It say 'smoking may be hazardous to your health.' "

203, 207, 458.

HEAVEN

377. A man had been very sick and died in the hospital. When he arrived at the Pearly Gates, St. Peter looked over his list and said, "We don't have your name on our list for today. Maybe you'd better try that other place?"

"Oh, no," the man said. "I lived a good life. I went to church, was kind to people, donated to the poor, tried to live by the Golden Rule. Please, St. Peter, don't turn me away. How about running my name through your computer again—maybe there's been a mistake."

So, St. Peter ran his name through his giant computer and in a few minutes he had an answer for the waiting man.

"Yes" he said, "your name is here after all. But, you're not due here for another three years. Who was your doctor, anyway?"

378. An avid football fan was chatting with his minister. "Do they have football in Heaven?" he asked.

"I don't know," the minister said.

"Well," the football fan said, "you are always talking to God. Next time, why don't you ask him? I'd like to know."

A few days later the minister called the man and said, "I did what you asked me. And I found out two things about it. First, they do have football in Heaven. And second, they told me that they have a ticket reserved for you on the forty-yard line for next week's big game."

HELP

379. A man traveling alone had stopped at a scenic mountain overlook to take a few pictures. Venturing too close to the edge of the precipice, he slipped and fell over. But, just before reaching the bottom of the 2,000 foot abyss, he grabbed a small tree that was growing out of a crevasse. Hanging on for dear life, he began to cry for help.

"Is anybody up there?" he called again and again. "Is anybody up there?"

After several hours his cry was answered. "Yes," a deep voice said, "I am up here. Can I help you?"

"You sure can," the man said. "Get a rope and rescue me."

"If you have faith," the voice said, "I can save you. Do you have faith?"

"Yes, I've got faith," the man yelled, "but hurry up before I fall."

"If you have faith," the voice said, "do as I say and you will be all right. Just let go of that tree you are holding onto and everything will be all right."

After a few moments of silence, the man cried out, "Is there anybody else up there?"

380. A rather weary housewife answered the phone. "Hey," a woman's voice said. "How are you today?"

"Oh, I feel terrible," the housewife said. "I'm tired. My back aches, my feet hurt. I've got a stack of ironing to do, the beds to make, and dishes to wash. The house is a mess. To tell you the truth, by the time I got the kids off to school this morning I was bushed. I don't think I can finish the day—it's that bad."

"Oh, that's terrible," her caller said. "I'll tell you what! You lie down and rest and I'll come over and help. I can do that ironing before you know it and then I'll get those dishes washed and the beds made. Besides, I have just baked a cake and I'll bring that along. How does that sound, Nancy?"

"Nancy?" the housewife said. "My name isn't Nancy. My name's Anne."

"Oh," said the caller. "I'm sorry. I thought I was talking to Nancy Thornton. I must have dialed the wrong number."

After a long silence, the housewife said with a note of sadness in her voice, "Does that mean you aren't coming over?"

226.

HENPECKED

381. The snow in Buffalo was three feet deep. The thermometer registered -12° F. Traffic was at a standstill. The manager of the donut shop was closing for the day when a lone customer fought his way to the front door. Half frozen to death the man said, "I want two donuts. One chocolate covered and one plain."

The donut man wrapped the donuts for the customer and said, "Do you mean to tell me you came out in this kind of weather just for two donuts? Who are they for?"

"They're for my wife," the customer said. "You don't think my mother would send me out on a night like this, do you?"

382. A man was so henpecked that his wife made him turn over his pay check to her every two weeks without cashing it. She cashed it and doled out his bus fare and lunch money each day. He was never allowed to spend a dime without her approval.

One day, when he came home from work he rushed in the front door and shouted, "Guess what! Guess what! I won, I won. I just won $50,000 dollars in the State Lottery!"

"That's wonderful," said his wife, "but just where did you get the money to buy a lottery ticket?"

110.

HITCH-HIKER

383. A tourist overtook a young man running beside the road and stopped and offered him a ride. "You seem to be in a big hurry," the tourist said. "Some kind of emergency?"

"No," the out-of-breath young man said, "I always do this when I want a ride. It works every time."

HOLD-UP

384. A man was stopped on a dark street by a man with a gun. "This is a stick-up," the man with the gun said. "Give me your money or I'll blow out your brains."

"Go ahead and shoot," the man said. "A person can live these days without brains, but not without money."

385. The manager of a restaurant had closed up for the night and was on his way to the midnight bank depository. As he walked toward his car in the parking lot a man emerged from the shadows.

"Don't worry," the shadowy figure said. "I'm just a panhandler. I need a little money. I haven't eaten in two days. I don't have any place to sleep. In fact, I have absolutely no earthly possessions in the world except this 38 automatic that's pointing at your stomach."

HONESTY

386. Some years ago a woman opened a tea room in Scranton. She selected an excellent location, advertised in the local newspaper, and before long her business was booming. Faced with spiraling inflation, she looked for ways to cut back on her basic costs and increase her profits.

She found that she could use her tea bags three times instead of only once, thereby saving quite a bit of money. She tried it. Soon her customers began to drift away. Finally, her business failed and she went bankrupt.

The moral to the story is: "Honest tea is the best policy."

387. The personnel director of a bank was interviewing applicants for the job of cashier. He called the former employer of one of the applicants to check his references.

"We are thinking of hiring your former employee as a cashier," the personnel director said. "I wonder if you could tell me whether or not he is perfectly honest."

"Honest," said the voice on the phone. "I should say he is. He has been arrested nine times for embezzlement, and he was found not guilty each time."

388. The used car salesman was in the final stages of closing a hot deal when he said to the man, "Have you ever heard anybody question my honesty?"

"No, I haven't," the prospective buyer said, "but on the other hand I have never heard anybody mention it either."

24, 103, 181, 263, 335, 336, 397, 544, 622, 660.

HORSES

389. A horse player stopped off at church on the way to the race track. Kneeling in prayer, he said, "Please, Lord, let me have a good day at the track today. Let me at least break even because I need the money to pay my rent."

390. The owner of a race horse was berating the jockey for losing the race. "I saw that hole open up in the final turn. Why didn't you ride through like you were supposed to do?"

"Sir," the jockey said, "did you ever try to ride through a hole that was moving faster than your horse?"

HOTEL

391. A man had tried to register at half a dozen hotels at a busy summer resort only to find that all rooms were taken. He was having the same experience at the last hotel on his list. "I'm sorry," the desk clerk said, "but we don't have one room left in the house. Everything has been booked for weeks."

"I know something about the hotel business," the would-be guest said. "I know that you always hold back a room or two for emergencies. Do you mean to tell me that if the President of the United States came in here right now, that you couldn't find a room for him?"

"I guess you are right," the room clerk said. "We'd strain a point and find something for the President."

"Fine," said the man, "give me his room. He won't be here. He's making a speech tonight in Peoria."

794, 795.

HUNTER

392. Two hunters were stalking big game in the Northwest wilds of Canada when they suddenly came across the footprints of a grizzly bear. One of the men said, "Look at those tracks. Quick, you start following them to see where he went. And I'll backtrack him to see where he came from."

459.

IDENTIFICATION

393. Two members of the Town Council began shouting at each other. "You are the biggest idiot in the world," the first man shouted.

"And you are the most bigoted and prejudiced donkey in town," the other man yelled.

The mayor, who was presiding, banged his gavel and said, "Quiet, gentlemen, quiet please. I'm afraid that in your excitement you have forgotten that I am in the room."

133, 742.

ILLNESS

394. The cruise ship had hit rough weather, and a number of the passengers had become sick. One man in particular seemed worse than the others as he leaned over the rail of the ship moaning and groaning. A steward, trying to offer a word of comfort, approached him and said, "Sir, we'll be in calm waters before you know it. Remember, nobody has ever died from seasickness."

"Oh, Oh, Oh," moaned the man. "Don't tell me that. It's only the hope of dying that is keeping me alive."

580.

INCOME TAX

395. The argument with the Internal Revenue agent ended this way: "That's just the point, sir: we *do* plan to make a federal case out of it."

396. As the three year old boy's grandmother was leaving after an afternoon visit, she gave the little fellow three shiny new dimes and told him to put them in his piggy bank. Half an hour later, the boy's mother heard the sound of coughing coming from the little boy's room. She rushed in to discover him red in the face and with one dime in his mouth. Realizing that he must have swallowed the other two dimes and that he was choking, she picked him up and rushed outside for help. Luckily, a motorist was passing and she hailed him.

"Help, help," she cried. "He's swallowed some money and I think he's choking to death."

"Don't worry, lady," the man said. "I'll take care of him." So saying, he grabbed the little fellow, turned him upside down and patted him on the back. Almost at once the little boy coughed up four dimes, two nickels and six pennies.

"Look at that," the woman cried. "He only swallowed two dimes and look at all that money. You must be a doctor."

"No, lady," the man said. "I work for the Internal Revenue Service."

397. The Internal Revenue Service received this letter:

"Three years ago I deliberately submitted a false Income Tax Return. Since then my conscience has bothered me so that I can't sleep well at night. Please apply the enclosed $20 on my past account although the forms do not indicate that I owe it."

At the bottom of the letter was this note: "PS: If I still can't sleep, I'll send the other $760 later."

398. A man had been charged by the Internal Revenue Service for non-payment of his income tax, and he had been hailed into court.

On the witness stand he said, "As God is my judge, I do not owe this tax."

The verdict from the judge was short: "He is not. I am. You do."

399. The minister answered his phone to hear a voice say, "This is the Internal Revenue Service. We're just checking on one of your member's tax return. Did a certain Gene Murphy give the church a $5,000 contribution last quarter?"

Thinking fast, the minister said, "The check hasn't arrived yet, but we'll have it within a few days—all I have to do is remind him of it."

400. The friend of a professor of mathematics saw him coming out of the office of a tax consultant.

"What were you doing there?" the friend asked.

"Arranging for them to do my income tax for me," the professor said.

"You?" the friend said. "You are a professor of mathematics. Do you mean to tell me that you can't fill out your own income tax forms?"

"That's right," the professor said. "It is beyond the abilities of a mathematician. It takes a magician."

401. The telephone company had been called to install extra equipment at the Internal Revenue Service for use during the last-minute April rush. When the installation man had finished his work he found an unoccupied desk and sat down to fill in his work order and write out his report. As he was working, an irate woman came into the office and walked over to him and said, "I want to talk to somebody about this income tax problem. I have had all kinds of trouble . . . ."

"Wait a minute, lady," the telephone man said. "I am not an IRS worker. You can see by the insignia on my jacket that I work for the telephone company. I am just here because I have been installing some extra telephones. You will have to talk to somebody else."

"Well," she said, "now that you are here, I might as well talk to you. Because I'm having trouble with the telephone company, too."

INDEPENDENCE

402. A hard-core individualist had reached the age of 65 and was filling in his application for Social Security. He came to the small box on the form which read, "Do Not Write in This Space."

With a red felt pen he wrote in that space, "I'll write where I damn well please."

403. The phone rang and when George answered it, a male voice said "Hi, George, are you ready to go to the poker game?"

"I can't go tonight," George said. "Something has come down here at the house."

"Come down?" the voice asked. "You mean come up, don't you?"

"No," George said. "It's my wife's foot."

INDIAN

404. The young generation of Indians was home from college for their Spring vacation. With special permission from the tribal council, they had brought in a rock and roll band and were having a real solid evening of dancing.

As the tempo picked up and the dance floor became crowded, one of the old timers sitting along the wall said to his squaw, "If that doesn't bring rain, nothing will."

405. "There I stood," said the man who was telling about his vacation adventures, "just a few miles out of Albuquerque face-to-face with Indians. As I turned to my right, there they were—Indians. Everywhere I looked, there were Indians—to my left and to my rear. Indians, Indians, Indians, closing in on me."

"My goodness," said a listener, "that was horrible. What did you do?"

"I did the only thing I could," the story teller said. "I bought a lot of Indian blankets, leather goods, and turquoise jewelry."

406. The Bloodmobile was stationed in front of the Indian trading post. Indians from all over the reservation were coming by to give blood.

A tourist who had done a bit of shopping in the trading post tried to start a conversation with a couple of young men standing in front.

"Are you a full-blooded Indian?" she asked one of the young men.

Pointing to the fellow standing beside him, the Indian said, "He is. But I'm not. I have just visited the Bloodmobile. I'm one pint short."

376, 759.

INFORMATION

407. A census taker had driven four miles down a remote country road in the performance of his duties. When he stopped his car in front of a mountain cabin, a woman sitting on the porch yelled at him, "We don't want any. We're not buying nothing."

"I'm not selling anything," the census taker said. "I'm here to take the census."

"We ain't got one," the woman said.

"You don't understand," the census taker said. "We're trying to find out how many people there are in the United States."

"Well," she said, "you sure wasted your time driving out here to ask me, because I don't know."

INGENUITY

408. The wholesale house for do-it-yourself plans received the following complaining letter: "Gentlemen: I built a bird house for the martins that come through here every Spring from a set of plans that you sent me. Your plans were no good. The bird house is too large, and besides, it keeps blowing out of the tree. I think you should refund the $4.00 that I paid you for those lousy plans. (Signed) Unhappy in Ohio."

By return mail the man received this letter. "Dear Unhappy in Ohio. We are sorry, but we sent you a set of plans for a sailboat by mistake. We apologize and are enclosing our check for $4.00 as you requested. If you think you are unhappy, you should have seen the letter we received from the man in Miami who came in last in the sailboat regatta trying to sail a leaky birdhouse."

409. Two women were reading the fashion magazines in the beauty parlor while waiting their turn to be served.

One woman said to the other, "Look, it says here that it takes seven Angora goats to make one of those new fluffy looking sweaters."

"My," said the other woman, "isn't it wonderful what they can teach animals to do these days."

187.

INSURANCE

410. An alert insurance salesman called on a young man shortly after he had returned from his honeymoon. "Now that you are married," he said, "I am sure that you will want to take out more insurance on yourself."

"I don't think I need any more," the young man said. "I don't think she is that dangerous."

411. A man called an insurance company and asked for information about hurricane insurance. "I realize the matter is too complicated to talk about on the phone," the man said. "So how about sending me a brochure and some advertising matter about the policy. Just put it in the mail. But don't send any salesmen to see me.

Please, no salesman."

Two days later a salesman from the insurance company delivered the material in person. "I don't want to talk to a salesman," the prospect said. "I distinctly said, no salesman."

The salesman, obviously in his early twenties and also obviously new on the job said, "That's why they sent me. I'm the nearest thing to 'no-salesman' they've got."

412. An auto store in a shopping center had been broken into and robbed, and the owner was chatting with a friend about it.

"That was a terrible thing," his friend said. "How much did you lose?"

"They took about $15,000 worth of merchandise," the store owner said. "But I guess we were lucky at that. It would have been a lot worse if he had broken into the store the night before."

"What difference would that have made?" his friend asked.

"Because," the store owner said, "just that morning we had marked everything in the store down 30% for our annual sale."

413. A widow was complaining about her former husband. "He didn't leave me one dime of insurance," she said. "All he left was a burial policy."

"Why," her friend said, "I heard that he left you the money to buy that beautiful diamond ring you are wearing."

"Oh," her friend said, "that was part of his burial policy. He left $2,000 for his casket and $3,000 for a stone. This is the stone."

460, 650, 651, 684.

INTERVIEW

414. Two reporters from the local newspaper were working as a team to find what the general population was thinking on various subjects. They rang the doorbell at one home, and one of them said to the man who came to the door, "We are from the newspaper. We would like to ask you several questions."

"Fine," he said, "what do you want to know?"

"First," said the reporter, "what concerns you the most as a citizen in today's troubled world?"

Without a moment's hesitation, he said, "The thing that concerns me the most right now is the fact that both of you are standing on my front porch which I just finished painting a half hour ago."

85, 456.

INTRODUCTION

415. The speaker had been introduced as "a man who is outstanding in his field."

He replied to that by saying, "When he said that, I hope he didn't mean that I reminded him of the farmer who was outstanding in his field because he was too stupid to come in out of the rain."

INVESTMENTS

416. A stock broker called one of his clients, a little old widow.

"I have good news for you," he said. "You own 500 shares of Sears Roebuck and they have just announced a split."

"That's too bad," she said, "after they have been together for so many years."

417. A mutual fund salesman was telephoning to make an appointment with a widow to discuss her investments.

"It will be all right for you to come to my home this evening," she said. "But I'm not sure about mutual funds. I have some municipals and some industrials. I'm afraid if you come this evening you're going to find me in a dilemma."

"Oh, that's all right," the salesman said. "The lady I called on last night was wearing a kimono."

JAYWALKING

418. Because it was drizzling rain, a man dashed across the street in the middle of the block. As he stepped under the

shelter of an awning, he came face to face with a policeman who began to write him a citation for jaywalking.

"Jaywalking!" the man shouted. "You can't write me a ticket for jaywalking. If you want to be technical about it, I wasn't walking, I was running."

"And if you want to be so technical," the policeman said, "I'm not writing, I'm printing."

JEALOUSY

419. A man who had just lost his job was chatting with a friend.

"Why did the foreman fire you?" the friend asked.

"Oh," the man said, "you know how foremen are. They're the fellows who stand around with their hands in their pockets watching everybody else work."

"Sure," the friend said. "Everybody knows that. But why did he fire you?"

"Jealousy," the man said. "All of the other workers thought I was the foreman."

JEWELER

420. A young lady stopped in a jewelry store and said to the jeweler, "My boyfriend gave me this ring for my birthday and I'm embarrassed because I'm not sure how to pronounce the name of the stone." She then put out her hand for the jeweler to see and asked, "Do you pronounce it 'turkoise' or 'turkwhoise'?"

The jeweler took a quick look and said that the proper way to pronounce it was "glass."

421. The young jewelry store clerk was getting married and was as nervous as most fellows under those circumstances. Everything ran smoothly until the minister came to the ring ceremony; then the groom's mind went completely blank.

"With this ring . . . ," prompted the minister in a whisper.

"With this ring," the young man said, "goes a money-back guarantee that it is a perfect three-quarter carat diamond mounted in platinum."

JUDGE

422. A group of judges were attending a convention meeting in Miami Beach. During one afternoon that was called "free time," several of them chartered a boat to do a bit of deepsea fishing. The Gulf Stream was rather rough that day, and one of the judges was leaning over the rail of the boat in great discomfort. One of the other judges, wanting to help, asked, "Is there anything I can do for you?"

"Yes," said the sick judge, "please overrule the motion."

423. The judge looked down from his bench at the old derelict and said, "You have been coming before me regularly for the past 10 years. I thought by this time that you would have amounted to something. You have been a great disappointment. Do you have anything to say for yourself?"

"Well, your honor," the old man said, "I feel pretty much the same way about you. I figured by this time you should be a member of the Supreme Court."

424. Two men had been fighting in back of the local pool room. Someone called the police, who arrested them and took them before the police judge.

"You two fellows should be ashamed of yourselves," the judge said. "You're grown men, not school kids. You should be able to settle your dispute without being brought into court."

"That's what we were trying to do," one of the men said, "when somebody called the police and they came and interfered."

425. A country bumpkin sort of fellow was elected Justice of the Peace in a backwoods town. Although he could count money, he had never learned to read and write much beyond being able to sign his name. Not being able to read the law and also not wanting people to know how ignorant he was, he developed a system of fining people—not from a law book but from a Sears Roebuck catalog.

One day a stranger, who was visiting a cousin in town, was picked up for speeding. When he was found guilty, the judge solemnly fingered through his catalog and fined the man $9.95.

The man was angry about the way he had been treated and was complaining about it to his cousin. His cousin said, "You're lucky. He fined you the price of a parasol for only $9.95. If he'd have turned the page he would have fined you $385 for a piano."

426. A judge was talking to his daughter about her new boyfriend. "I've told you before, I think that fellow is no good. He's shiftless and lazy and isn't fit for you to go with."

"I've heard all that before," his daughter said. "And I told him what you said about him."

"What did he say?" the judge asked.

"He said that wasn't the first wrong judgment you've ever made."

427. A man had been arrested and charged with car theft. The judge was explaining his rights.

"You have a choice," the judge said. "You can be tried in my court by me alone. Or you can be transferred to the District Court and be tried by a jury of your peers."

"What are peers?" the man asked.

"Peers are people who are your equals. People like you. The kind of people you associate with, live with, do business with."

"In that case," the man said, "I'd rather be tried by you. I sure don't want to be tried by a bunch of car thieves."

428. The judge looked sternly at the man accused of driving under the influence of alcohol. "The last time you were here," said the judge, "I thought I told you I didn't want to see you here again."

"That's what I tried to tell the patrolman," the man said, "but he arrested me anyway."

429. A man had been arrested for wife-beating. The judge said to the prosecuting attorney, "This man is charged with beating his wife with an oak leaf. How could anyone beat someone with an oak leaf?"

"It was an oak leaf from the dining room table," the prosecutor said.

7, 201, 203, 204, 398, 440, 588, 591, 729, 816.

JURY

430. The man had been charged with stealing watermelons, and the small-town jury was reading the verdict. "We find the defendant guilty. We don't think he stole the watermelons because we don't think he was there, but we know him and we are sure he would have stolen them if he had half a chance."

603.

JUSTICE

431. A poor Georgia sharecropper was arrested for stealing. When his case came before the court, the clerk called out, "The State of Georgia versus Jack Jackson."

"Listen to that," the man said to his court-appointed lawyer. "Six million people against me just for stealing three chickens."

432. The little five year old girl came crying to her mother. "Billy took the biggest piece of cake," she said. "And it's not fair because he was eating cake three years before I was born."

KINDERGARTEN

433. This was the little boy's first day at kindergarten. His teacher was filling in his personal record card and was asking him the usual questions. "Have you ever had the measles, or chicken pox or mumps?" she asked.

"No ma'am," the little fellow said, "all I've ever had is Rice Krispies and Frosted Flakes."

434. The little boy had attended kindergarten for the first time, and his father was chatting with him about it. "What did you learn today?"

"I learned to say 'yes, sir' and 'no, sir'," he said.

"You did?" asked his father.

"Uh-huh," the little fellow said.

435. The teacher was getting acquainted with her new class on the first day of kindergarten. She said to one little girl, "And what does your father do?"

"What my mother tells him to," the little girl said.

75.

LABOR

436. The newspaper reporter was interviewing the head of the union that had gone out on strike.

"What is it that you want?" the reporter asked.

"More," was the terse reply.

LAWYER

437. A lawyer in an accident case was cross examining a witness who happened to be the proverbial little old lady. "Isn't it true," he asked, "that after the accident, the driver made only a cursory examination of his damaged car?"

"That's right," the witness said. "He sure did. In fact it was so cursory that it embarrassed everyone who heard him and I had to put my hands over my ears to keep from hearing him."

438. A lawyer was talking to his son about going to college. "I assume you plan to follow my profession and study law," he said.

"Not really, Dad," his son said. "I'v given the problem a lot of thought. I think I would rather study medicine. Doctors are more important than lawyers."

"Doctors more important than lawyers?" his father shouted. "Where did you ever get that stupid idea?"

"It's not so stupid," his son said. "Did you ever hear anybody at a football game stand up and shout 'is there a lawyer here?' "

439. A Chicago lawyer was trying to find a young woman who had inherited a fortune. He had traced her as far as Los Angeles, but there her trail ended. He flew West and hired a local detective agency to help him find her. The agency placed the case in the hands of one of their cleverest investigators. He was young and handsome and had a reputation for hard work.

Several weeks went by without a word when one day the lawyer received a telephone call from the investigator. "The young lady has been located," he told the lawyer.

"Wonderful," the lawyer said. "Where is she?"

"Here at my place," the young detective said. "We were married yesterday."

440. The lawyer was examining the witness. "Isn't it true," he shouted, "that you were given $200 to throw this case?"

The witness did not answer. Instead, he just stared out the window as though he had not even heard the question. The lawyer repeated the question with the same reaction—no response.

Finally, the judge said to the witness, "Please answer the question."

"Oh," said the witness with much surprise in his voice, "I thought he was talking to you."

441. A man called on his lawyer and said, "I want to sue that man who lives across the street from me. He called me a hippopotamus."

"We can do that," the lawyer said. "When did he call you that?"

"Six years ago," the man said.

"Six years ago?" the lawyer said. "Why have you waited so long to file suit against him?"

"Well," the man said, "yesterday I took the kids to the zoo and it was the first time I had ever seen a hippopotamus."

7, 17, 205, 465, 562.

LAZINESS

442. The repair truck from the appliance company drove into the front yard. When the housewife answered the door the repairman said, "I understand you've got something here that doesn't work. Is that right?"

"Yes," the woman answered. "He's asleep in his hammock on the patio."

443. The husband had been lying in his back yard hammock all afternoon taking life easy. He had been reading a book about the life of Napoleon, and as he put the book aside he rolled over and said to his wife, who was raking the yard, "Do you know what I would have done if I had been Napoleon?"

"Yes, I do," his wife shouted at him. "You would have loafed all day long in the back yard of your farm in Corsica and let it grow up with weeds while Mrs. Napoleon waited on you hand and foot and raked the leaves."

444. A tourist drove into a small town and spoke to a man who was sitting on a bench in front of the post office.

"How long have you lived here?" the tourist asked.

"About 40 years," the native said.

"It sure is an out-of-the-way place, isn't it?" the tourist asked."

"It sure is," the native said.

"There isn't much going on," the tourist said. "I don't see anything here to keep you busy."

"Neither do I," the man said. "That's why I like it."

148, 308.

LIAR

445. Two women were talking. "I think my husband has been lying to me lately," the first one said.

"Can't you tell when he's lying?" her friend asked. "I can tell when my husband is lying to me."

"How can you tell?" the first one asked.

"It's easy," said her friend. "I look in his eyes, then I look at his lips. If his lips are moving, he's lying."

95, 305, 336, 778, 781.

LIBRARY

446. The first grader had not developed proper library manners and was talking rather loudly and disturbing everyone near him. The librarian went over to him and said, "Sh! Please be quiet. The people near you can't read."

"They can't read?" he exclaimed. "Then what are they doing here?"

LIGHT

447. The professor of poetry was trying to inspire his class to become creative. "I want you to meditate on this line of poetry," he said. "It is one of the most though provoking ideas ever written. This is it. 'Walk with light.' Isn't that a profound thought? 'Walk with light.' I want you to think about it for a few moments and tell me what it means to you."

One student held up his hand, and when he was given permission to speak, said, "That's what the sign says down at the traffic light, and to me it means I'm supposed to be careful crossing the street."

LISTENING

448. A church had installed a new set of electronic chimes in their church steeple. They were set to spread the sound of sacred music throughout the neighborhood each Sunday afternoon. Following the dedication of the chimes on the first Sunday they were in use, the minister sent a dozen or more of his members to get the reaction of the people living nearby.

As the chimes were playing, the members began ringing doorbells and asking their questions. As one lady came to her door, a church member said, "Hello. I'm from the church and I wanted to find out . . . ."

"What did you say?" the lady asked.

The church member said, "I said I'm from the church and . . . ."

"What?" the woman shouted.

Raising her voice, the woman from the church said, "I am from the church and . . . ."

"You'll have to shout," the lady said. "I can't hear a word you are saying on account of those damn chimes."

449. A man was visiting an old friend on his farm in Kentucky. While they were sitting on the front porch drinking mint juleps, a half dozen of the farmer's hounds flushed a fox and took off through the woods after him. As the sound of their barking filled the air, the farmer closed his eyes and said, "Listen to that music. Did you ever hear a more beautiful symphony in all your life?"

His visitor looked perplexed and said, "I'm sorry but I can't hear anything because of those damn dogs."

161.

LITTLE BOY

450. There were 10 children in the family. The older ones took care of the younger ones. One morning, the three-year-old appeared fully dressed at the breakfast table before anyone else.

"How did you get dressed so fast?" his father asked.

"Well," said the little one, "they never undressed me last night."

451. "I'm sorry," the kid said to his friend, "I can't come out to play right now. I've got to stay in and help my Dad with my homework."

452. The little first grader appeared to be greatly upset when he came to the principal's office and asked if he might use the telephone to call his mother.

"Is there something the matter?" the principal asked. "Can I help you?"

"Well," the little fellow said, "yesterday I forgot my sweater and left it here at school. This morning my mother told me not to come home without it. I can't find it anywhere and I want to call her on the phone and ask her where she wants me to go."

9, 141, 196, 307, 367, 433, 710.

LITTLE GIRL

453. The little girl was four years old. She had reached the point where her mother and father were very careful about what they said around her for fear she would go about the neighborhood repeating things she shouldn't.

One afternoon, her grandmother came to visit. As her grandmother was removing her coat she said to the little girl,

"Well, it's good to see you again. What's new around here since I was here last time?"

"How should I know?" the little girl said, "they spell everything."

454. Grandmother said to the little four year old, "They tell me you have been a good little girl. And I'll tell you what I am going to do. I'm going to give you a brand new bright shiny penny."

"If it's all the same to you," the kid said, "I'd rather have a dirty old dime."

102, 249, 296, 357, 365, 396, 432, 576, 664, 731.

LONGEVITY

455. A man who was celebrating his 100th birthday was being interviewed on television. The anchor man asked, "To what do you owe your longevity?"

"Nothing to it," the old man said. "Anybody can do it. I just keep breathing."

456. The newspaper reporter was interviewing the nonagenarian. "Have you lived in this part of the country all of your life?" he asked.

"Not yet," the wise old fellow said, "but I sure hope to."

457. The reporter was interviewing the old man on his 100th birthday. "What do you think of modern-day women?" the young fellow asked.

"I can't help you with that question," the old man said, "because I quit thinking about women nearly three years ago."

458. The TV reporter had been interviewing the old man on his 100th birthday. As the program came to a close, he shook hands with the old man and said, "Once again, happy birthday. I hope to see you right here again next year."

"I see no reason why not," the old fellow said. "You look healthy enough to me."

21, 23, 90, 685.

LOST

459. For several hours the hunting party had wandered in circles, and now that night was coming on, it was obvious that they were lost.

"You told us you were the greatest guide in the state of Montana," one of the hunters shouted at the guide.

"I am," the guide said, "but I think we are in Canada."

133.

LOVE

460. A man in his early sixties had just married a widow in her late forties. Figuring that the law of averages would hold and that he would die before she would, he was explaining what property he had and what his estate would come to when he passed away.

"First, about the insurance," he said. "I carry only one policy. It's for $75,000."

"I hate to hear you talking like that," his bride said. "I want to think only of us living together for a long, long time. By the way, is that $75,000 straight life or does it carry a double indemnity clause in case of accident?"

461. Two friends who lived in the West Virginia mountains were chatting one day. "Horace," the first one said, "why didn't you ever get married?"

"I thought about it several times," Horace said, "but things just didn't work out. The first girl I wanted to marry was a pretty little thing with red hair, but my mother didn't like the way she talked. My second girlfriend was a cute little blonde who sang in a hillbilly band, but when I brought her home my mother didn't like her looks. Then I tried to find a girl who would please my mother. I finally found a young lady down in Charleston who looked exactly like my mother. She talked like my mother and even walked like her. I was sure she'd be able to please my mother. But things went wrong again. So, I gave up the idea."

"What went wrong that last time?" his friend asked. "Didn't your mother like her?"

"Oh, yes, Mother thought she was perfect," said the would-be groom, "but my Dad couldn't stand the sight of her."

462. "I'm not rich and I don't own a new car and a yacht and a winter home in Florida like Jack Hodges," the young man said to his girlfriend, "but I love you from the bottom of my heart."

"I love you, too," his girlfriend said, "but while we are chatting about it, tell me more about Jack Hodges."

272, 319, 473, 636, 637, 745.

LOYALTY

463. The huge crowd at the football game had been giving the referee a bad time all afternoon. They heckled him over every close decision he made. When the game was over and he was driving home with his wife he said, "Honey, I like you to attend these games, but I think maybe from now on you should stay at home when I referee. It must have been terribly embarrassing for you when everyone stood up and booed me this afternoon."

"Well, not really," she said, "because when they did, I stood up and booed as loud as they did."

124, 320, 329. 536.

LUCK

464. A man was playing roulette and was down to his last chip. As he stood undecided about what to do with it, he heard a wee voice whisper in his ear, "Play 32." So, figuring he probably would lose it anyway, he played 32—and won.

The little voice then whispered, "Put it all on 8."

He did. And he won again.

"Now, let it all ride on 19," the little voice said. The player followed the advice of the little voice and won a third time.

"Here we go for the last time," the little voice said, "and your fortune. Put all of it on 3."

The man did as he was told. As the little white ball snuggled down in the 15 slot, the man heard the little voice say, "Aw shucks. That's the way it goes."

MAIL

465. A lady went into the post office to buy stamps to mail her daughter's wedding invitations.

"I'd like 200 stamps, please," she said to the clerk.

"What denomination?" the clerk asked.

"Oh, dear," she said. "I didn't know it had come to that. I suppose it would be best if I split them. Give me 100 Baptist and 100 Presbyterian."

478.

MANNERS

466. The little girl came in from the back yard and said to her mother, who was preparing dinner, "Can I have a cookie?"

"How do you ask for it?" her mother said.

"May I have a cookie?" the little girl said.

"What do you say when you ask for something?" her mother said.

"May I please have a cookie?" she said.

"No," her mother said. "It's too near dinner time. It will spoil your appetite."

MARRIAGE

467. Two men met for the first time since they had roomed together in college. "It sure has been a long time," the first fellow said. "Did you ever marry the girl you were going with, or do you still sew on your own buttons and do your own cooking and vacuuming?"

"Yes," his old friend said.

468. One young lady said to her friend, "Joe and Mabel are only half serious about getting married."

"What do you mean, half serious?" her friend asked

"Mabel is. Joe isn't."

469. Two secretaries who worked on Capitol Hill in Washington, D.C., and knew the ways of the congressmen, were chatting.

"I'll tell you the kind of man I want to marry," said one of the girls. "I want a man who will treat me as if I were a voter and he were a candidate for office."

470. The minister had reached that portion of the marriage ceremony where he said, ". . . and do you take this woman for better or for worse, for richer or for poorer, through sickness and in health, in good times and in bad, in . . "

"Please," whispered the bride almost in tears, "if you aren't careful, you're going to talk him out of it."

471. A man was telling his troubles to a marriage counselor. "My wife and I were perfectly happy for 25 years," he said.

"In that case," the counselor asked, "what has caused all of your troubles?"

"We met," the man said.

472. A man and his wife had just moved to Sarasota when he had a heart attack and died. His brother flew in from up North for the funeral. Because his wife had just died three months before, he and his brother's widow leaned on each other for comfort from their grief. Within a week they had fallen in love. Two weeks later they were married and the new husband moved to Sarasota.

The woman realized that her remarriage was rather hasty, and to ease her conscience she had a color portrait of her former husband framed and placed on the piano.

Shortly after that some new neighbors dropped by, and they asked who the man in the picture was.

"Oh," the woman said, "that's my brother-in-law. He died about three months ago."

473. "Why have you made up your mind to marry a rich girl?" a man asked his friend.

"Because," said the friend, "I will then be able to give my wife everything that her money can buy."

474. A man and his wife were talking about two men who had been in the news recently.

"I knew them both," the husband said. "They were friends. One of them was a ne'er do well. He never held a steady job, never amounted to anything. The other fellow worked hard, saved his money, invested it properly, and planned for the future. When he died, he left his widow more than two million dollars."

"Yes," his wife said. "I read that in the paper. I also see by the paper where the ne'er do well is going to marry his friend's widow."

475. The young man had approached the father of his girlfriend and asked permission to marry her.

"I don't want my daughter tied down to a stupid nincompoop for the rest of her life," the girl's father said.

"Thank you, sir," the you man said. "We knew you would give us your consent."

576. The mountaineer had arranged to marry the 14 year old girl. The wedding day was set. He was chatting to a friend about it. "I've got a problem. I don't know whether to take her on a honeymoon or send her to school."

34, 39, 107, 247, 330, 332, 334, 369, 421, 461, 610, 637, 640, 674, 819, 820.

MARTINI

477. A dedicated martini drinker ordered his favorite drink. He explained to the bartender that he wanted it made twenty-to-one. As the bartender carefully complied with the customer's wishes, he said, "Do you want me to twist a bit of lemon peel over it?"

"No," the customer shouted. "If I had wanted a lemonade, I would have ordered one."

302.

MAYOR

478. A friend was sitting in the Mayor's office while he was opening his mail. "Look at this letter," the Mayor said. "It's addressed to 'The Stupidest Man in Town.' "

"A man should have better sense than to write a letter like that," the Mayor's friend said. "Why, you would get mad at him before you even read his letter."

"Oh," said the Mayor. "I wouldn't get mad over a letter like that. But it does upset me when I realize that the post office knew where to deliver it."

MEMBERSHIP

479. In the old days before motels, when traveling salesmen stayed in boarding houses, a man knocked on what appeared to be such a place and said to the woman who came to the door, "Do you take lodgers?"

"That depends," she said. "What lodge do you belong to?"

MEMORY

480. A woman, who was obviously in her fifties, had just moved to town and was visiting the local clinic for the first time. "I just need a complete checkup," she told the doctor.

Before the doctor sent her through the routine of the clinic, he asked her a number of questions for his permanent records.

"What symptoms do you have?" he asked.

"I'm not too well," she said. "I have pains in my wrists, and I don't sleep well because of a backache, and I seem to have a constant head cold, and I see spots in front of my eyes, and I have periodic headaches."

The doctor made a lot of notations on his chart and then said, "And how old are you?"

The woman tried to look demure and said, "Thirty-two."

The doctor filled in her age as she gave it to him, but right beside it had added another symptom that the woman had not mentioned. He wrote, "Slight loss of memory."

481. A man visited a psychiatrist. "I have a terrible problem," he said. I think I'm losing my memory. Do you think you can help me?"

"Yes," said the psychiatrist, "I have helped on cases of this kind. We never can be sure, but we can try." He then suggested that his patient sit in a large reclining chair and get as comfortable as possible.

"Now," said the psychiatrist, "just relax and tell me all about your problem."

The man immediately sat up and stared wild-eyed at the doctor and asked with great surprise in his voice, "What problem?"

323, 772.

MINISTER

482. A minister was called to come to the bedside of a man who was dying. In spite of the lateness of the hour, the minister came and did what he could for the dying man.

As he was leaving, the minister said to the man's wife, "I was happy to come and comfort your husband the best I could. But, you are not members of my church. I just wondered if you don't have a church affiliation. Don't you have a minister of your own faith?"

"Oh, yes," the woman said, "but we wouldn't call him out in the middle of the night and have him exposed to scarlet fever."

483. A minister put an advertisement in the paper for a handyman. The next morning a well-dressed young man came to the door.

"Can you start a fire and have breakfast ready by 7:00?"

The young man said he thought he could.

"Can you polish the silver, wash the dishes and keep the house picked up and the lawn mowed?" the minister asked him.

"Look," said the young man, "I came to make arrangements for my wedding, but if it is going to be anything like that, I have decided to forget the whole thing."

484. A minister was stopped on the Interstate for speeding. As most people do, he wanted to argue with the patrolman about how fast he was going. "I sure wasn't going 70 miles an hour," he said. "How did you time my speed? I don't see a radar any place."

"We didn't catch you with radar," the patrolman said. "You were spotted and timed by our helicopter patrol."

"Oh," said the minister. "That's all right then, because I never question anything that comes from above."

485. A minister's wife who had missed his sermon because of a touch of the flu asked him about the morning service. "What did you preach about?"

"My sermon today called on the rich to give to the poor," he said.

"Did it go over well with the congregation?" she asked.

"About fifty-fifty," he said. "I convinced the poor."

486. The clock had just struck 3:00 A.M. when the minister's teenager daughter returned from a dance. He and his wife had been waiting up for the girl, and as she came in the front door, he said to her rather scornfully, "Good morning, child of the devil."

Speaking sweetly, as any child should, she said, "Good morning, father."

487. A man had stolen a turkey, and because of his conscience, he visited his minister. "My family was hungry," the man said. "So I stole this turkey. But I feel that I have sinned. Would you please take it."

"Certainly not," the minister said.

"Then what should I do with it?" the man asked.

"Give it back to the man you stole it from," the minister said.

"I offered it to him," the man said. "But he refused it. Now what should I do?"

"In that case," the minister said, "it would be all right for you to keep it and feed your family."

That seemed to settle things as far as the man was concerned. He said, "Thank you for you help, sir." He picked up the turkey and hurried away.

Later that afternoon when the minister returned home, he discovered that somebody had stolen his Thanksgiving turkey.

354, 399, 658.

MISTAKE

488. Computers are great. They make lots of mistakes, but when they do, it's nobody's fault.

38, 304, 323, 494.

MODERN GENERATION

489. The bridge game had stopped while the hostess went to the kitchen to fix some refreshments. She said to her little five year old girl, "You go in the front room and chat with the ladies while I get things ready."

Dutifully, the little girl did as she was told. To say the least, she was not very attractive. Her teeth were misshapen, she was popeyed and freckled faced and her hair was stringy. One of the guest leaned over to her friend and said, "It's a pity isn't it?" Then she spelled out the rest of her sentence: "S-h-e i-s n-o-t v-e-r-y p-r-e-t-t-y i-s s-h-e?"

But, before the other woman could spell out her agreement, the little girl said, "That's right, but she sure is s-m-a-r-t."

MODERN MUSIC

490. The teenager had just put on the latest hit album and turned the hi-fi to full volume when her father came in the front door.

"Oh, Dad," she shouted. "Listen to that. Did you ever in your life hear anything to equal it?"

"Only once," he shouted back. "When I was a boy a truck loaded with milk cans hit another truck loaded with ducks."

MODERN TECHNOLOGY

491. Through technology, man has been able to make a 25¢ cold drink can that will last forever and a $16,000 automobile that will rust away in five years.

139.

MONASTERY

492. A monastery in California had been so successful with their winery that hundreds of vacationers visited it every day. With a keen eye for making money, they decided to set up a small cafe or tearoom. After much discussion they agreed that it should be a fish and chips place.

The first day it was open, a smart aleck visitor said to the monk who was acting as the cashier. "The fish and chips were delicious. Are you by any chance the fish friar?"

"No," he replied, "I'm the chip monk."

MONEY

493. Two Arabs entered a large New York bank. One was obviously the servant of the other because he was not as elegantly dressed and he was struggling with a huge suitcase.

The well dressed Arab said he would like to open an account and was ushered to the proper bank official.

"I would like to open a checking account," the Arab said. "I have three million dollars in cash as my initial deposit."

The bank official was delighted, and he called on several of his tellers to help count the money and make out the deposit slip and the bank book. After half an hour, the bank official said to the Arab, "I'm sorry, sir, but there seems to be some mistake. There were only two million dollars in your suitcase."

Horrified, the Arab shouted at his servant, "You stupid camel, you brought the wrong suitcase."

494. Two secretaries were chatting over lunch.

"All you think about is money," said the first.

"No it isn't," her friend said. "I think of men, too."

"What kind of men?"

"Men with money, of course."

495. A teenager had asked his father if he could use the family car and also if he could have five dollars.

"Don't you realize that there are more important things than money?" his father asked.

"Yes," his son said, "but you've got to have money to take them to the movies and buy them a hamburger afterwards."

496. The little boy's grandmother had given him a nickel and he went to the drug store to spend it.

"Give me an ice cream cone, please," he said to the clerk as he laid down his nickel.

"Ice cream cones are a dime now," the clerk said.

"Okay," the little fellow said. "Give me a candy bar."

"They are 10 cents, too," the clerk said.

"Then I guess I'll take a package of chewing gum," the boy said.

"Chewing gum costs seven cents now," the clerk said.

With that, the little fellow turned and started out the door.

"Wait a minute," called the clerk, "You forgot your nickel."

"Keep it," the little fellow said. "It won't buy anything."

497. The young man asked his father for five dollars to take his girlfriend to a school dance.

"Here's the five dollars," his father said, "but for goodness sakes make it go as far as you can."

And his son's quick reply was, "Dad, I'll make that five dollars go so far that you'll never see any of it again."

498. Two men were chatting about a friend. "What in the world did Joe do with all of his money? Three or four years ago he inherited a small fortune from an aunt and now I understand he is flat broke."

"That's right," his friend said. "He ran through a pot of money. He spent most of it on whiskey and women and the rest of it he spent foolishly."

499. Two men were chatting about a friend. "I understand his parents were wealthy, but he doesn't seem to be rich himself."

"That's right," the other fellow said. "When he was a baby, they hired a nursemaid to look after him. Every afternoon she would wheel him through the park in his baby carriage. And he has never got over it. He's been pushed for money ever since."

500. Two men, vacationing with their families, were riding the steamboat at Disneyworld. One said to the other, "I wish I had enough money to buy a steamboat."

"What?" his friend said. "We live in the middle of Kansas. There isn't any water for miles and miles. What do you want with a steamboat?"

"I don't want a steamboat," the man said. "I just wish I had enough money to buy one."

42, 328, 384, 454, 473, 610, 641, 675, 713, 715, 730.

MOTHER

501. "My mother does bird imitations," bragged a little boy.

"Name one," his friend said.
"She watches me like a hawk," the first kid said.

502. A mother was having difficulty persuading her son to go to school one morning.

He was standing at the front door crying and said, "Nobody at school likes me. The teachers don't like me, and the kids all pick on me. The bus driver hates me, the County Superintendent wants to transfer me to another school. Even the janitor won't have anything to do with me. And I'm not going to school today."

"But," his mother said, "you've got to go. You are a big boy. You're strong. And you have a lot to learn. You want to show everybody that you are a leader. Besides, you are 42 years old. You're the principal. You've got to go."

503. One Sunday afternoon the six-year-old's father was showing her the photographs of her parents' wedding. He was telling her what a wonderful day it was with all of the ceremony and the friends who had gathered to wish them well.

"Oh," said the little girl, "that's the day when mother came to work for us, wasn't it?"

150, 196, 357, 381.

MOTHER-IN-LAW

504. A couple who had been married for 10 years decided they would like a second honeymoon. Because both of them had been working, this would be the first time they had been away from home together since their wedding day.

As they were sitting in the dining room discussing their plans, the husband kept glancing into the living room where a little old lady sat in front of the TV knitting.

"Our biggest problem, as I see it," he said, "is what we are going to do about your mother while we are away."

"My mother!" his wife cried. "I thought she was your mother."

40, 686.

MOTION PICTURES

505. A minister was speaking to a civic group against the modern trend toward sexy movies. "Look at the filth they are giving us," he cried. "A mistress kills her lover because he goes home to his wife. Then she drives 90 miles an hour through city traffic in a convertible—stark naked. Then the police take out after her and 12 of their cars end up in a huge crash that catches fire and sets fire to a hotel; and all the people in the hotel run out at three o'clock in the morning without any clothes on. What do you make of that kind of movie?"

A voice in the back said, "Where's it playing?"

MOTIVATION

506. Several new members of the parachute jumping club were standing in line to receive their parachutes. Standing nearby was an obvious senior-citizen who was wearing the insignia of the club. Eager to be friendly, one of the new members asked, "What made you decide to become a jumper?"

"A C-47 with two dead engines," the old-timer said.

MUSIC

507. At a University of Kentucky class reunion, an alumnus who had become a night club singer was called on to sing "My Old Kentucky Home." Being a bit exuberant due to too much bourbon, he really threw himself into the song. As his voice rose to dramatic pitch, another classmate sat in the front row and began to weep. A friend said to him, "I had no idea you were so sentimental. Are you a Kentuckian?"

"No," he said, "I'm a musician."

508. The lady answered the doorbell to see a quiet looking little man standing there with a black bag in his hand. "I've come to tune your piano," he said.

"We have a piano," she said, "but I didn't call anybody to tune it."

"I know," he said, "but your neighbors did."

448, 449.

MUSICIAN

509. A man went to see a real estate salesman and said, "I want a house that is in the country. It should be at least a mile from the nearest neighbor."

"I understand what you want," the real estate salesman said. "You are planning to practice the simple life. Is that it?"

"No," the man said, "I plan to practice the trombone."

510. A woman had just received her final divorce decree from a song writer and was chatting with a friend about it. "He was terrible," she said. "At first he seemed so loving and understanding and romantic with his songs, but he turned out to be a tyrant."

"Well," said her friend. "I hate to say I told you so, but I said time and time again that you shouldn't marry him. Everybody knows that song writers make the world's worst husbands."

Six months later, the divorcee fell in love and married another song writer. The next day she received this message with a bouquet of roses from her former husband: "Congratulations and best wishes for a happy marriage.(Signed), The Frying Pan."

MYSTERY

511. A young fellow was bragging to his girlfriend about his new car.

"It's the quietest running car you ever saw," he said. "You can't hear it. Even when you are sitting in it with the engine running, you can't hear it."

"Wonderful," his girlfriend said.

"Not only that," he bragged, "there's no vibration. You can't feel it when it's running."

"Wonderful."

"And it has that new burner that burns up all the gas so that you can't smell it, either," he said.

"Wonderful."

"And when you open it up," he said, "Swish—down the road. You can't see it, it's so fast. How does all that sound?"

"It sounds wonderful," she said, "but, like I keep saying, if you can't hear it, or feel it, or smell it or see it, how do you know it's there?"

665.

NAGGING

512. "Quit rushing me!" the wife yelled downstairs to her husband. "I told you half an hour ago I'd be ready in five minutes. And when I say five minutes, I mean five minutes."

NAME

513. "Is this your package?" the delivery man asked. "This is the right address but the name is obliterated."

"In that case it isn't my package," the man said. "My name is O'Flaherity."

514. A new restaurant had opened up across the street from the bank, and one of the tellers began to eat breakfast there several times a week. After the third or fourth week, as he was paying his check, the cashier spoke to him in a friendly manner and said, "Good morning, Mr. Willingham. We hope you enjoyed your breakfast."

The man's name was Bergman, but he didn't correct the cashier because he didn't want to embarrass her in front of other people waiting in line to pay. However, every morning after that she would call him "Mr. Willingham."

After a week of that, he finally spoke to her when nobody was near and told her his name was Bergman—Dave Bergman.

He thought he had the problem taken care of until the next morning when he went to pay his check. This time the young lady said, "Good morning, Mr. Willingham. Do you know there's a man who eats in here now and then who looks exactly like you. His name is Dave Bergman."

515. Two cowboys met in a bar. "Call me Tex," the first one said as they shook hands.

"Hey," said the other one. "That's my name, too. All my friends call me Tex."

"You from Texas?" the first cowboy asked.

"No," the second cowboy said, "I'm from Louisiana but I sure don't want to be called Louise. Are you from Texas?"

"No," said the first cowboy. "but I like to be called Tex for the same reason. I'm from Maryland."

"That makes three of us," said another cowboy who had been eavesdropping on the conversation. "I'm from Virginia."

116, 122, 368, 369, 393.

NATIVE

516. A woman visiting a zoo was being shown around by a guide. They came to a cage occupied by a kangaroo.

"Here, lady," he said, "we have a native of Australia."

"Good gracious," she said, "and to think my aunt married one of them."

NATURE

517. The teacher was trying to teach the children a bit of geography. "Tell me, Jack, where are elephants found."

"Gosh," he said, "they are so big, I didn't know any of them ever got lost."

NAVY

518. Two young men who were being discharged from the Navy were chatting.

The first fellow said to his friend, "Now that you have served four years in the Navy, what do you think of the sea?"

"I'll tell you what I think of it," his friend said. "When I leave here today I'm going to put an oar over my shoulder and start walking down the road. I'm going to walk and walk and walk until somebody stops me and asks me what I've got over my shoulder. Then I'm going to settle down right there until I die."

756.

NEWLYWEDS

519. A newlywed was complaining to her mother, "Marriage really is a terrible grind. I never dreamed it would be like this. You wash dishes, make the beds, tidy up the living room and then two weeks later you have to do it all over again."

NEWS

520. A woman was chatting with a friend about her husband. "He used to take the evening news on television with a grain of salt. Now, it's so bad, he takes it with five milligrams of Valium."

328.

NEWSPAPER

521. An excellent example of slanted journalism came in a small town weekly that reported the results of a horse race at the county fair. Only two horses were entered in the race. One was owned by a local friend of the editor named Darrell Brown. The winner belonged to a man named Colburn who lived in the next county. Colburn's horse won the race. Without mentioning that only two horses ran, the news account read as follows: "Brown's horse came in second and Colburn's horse came in next to last."

257, 746.

NICKNAMES

522. Nicknames get started in the oddest ways. The boys in the second grade started calling one of the girls "Pretty." After a few days of that, she got mad and shouted at them, "Quit calling me that. My name is not pretty."

So, from then on they called her "Not-Pretty."

523. A college freshman was filling in his registration form. In addition to asking for such information as his address and phone number, he came to this question, "Nicknames or other names by which you receive mail."

He thought for a moment and wrote, "Occupant."

524. A young man had filled in his application for employment. Where it asked his name (last name first, first name last), he had put, "Johnson, Hubert." Where it asked for his nickname, if any, he had put, "Shot, Hot."

525. Two teachers were chatting about their students. "Kids are funny," the first one said. "They like to give each other nicknames. A boy in my class is named Will Knot and they call him Won't."

The other teacher agreed and said, "I have a boy named Nosmo King and the other kids call him No Smoking."

NIGHT CLUB

526. The reservations girl at the swank restaurant and night club answered the phone.

"I would like to make reservations for six for tonight. Do you have a cover charge or a minimum?"

"We don't have a cover charge," the young lady said, "but we do have a minimum. That's $12 per person."

"What about children?" the caller asked. "We have four children. Do they get half price?"

"No," the young lady explained. "The minimum is the same for everybody."

"But," the caller insisted, "the airlines only charge half fare for children."

"That sounds like a good idea," the young lady said. "Why don't you put the kids on a plane and you and your wife come and enjoy the dinner and show without them?"

913.

NURSE

527. A man had been confined in the hospital for several weeks because of a compound fracture of his leg. During that time, he had fallen in love with his nurse and she seemed to have fallen in love with him.

As the day drew near for him to leave the hospital, he said to her, "I'm so in love with you, darling. I really don't want to leave. I'd like to stay here forever."

"You might get your wish," she said, "because the head surgeon is in love with me too, and he saw you kissing me last night."

213.

OCCUPATION

528. The first grade teacher was having "show and tell." Today the children were telling about their fathers. One little girl said her father was a lawyer, another said hers was a plumber, and a little boy said his father worked in a bank.

"And what does your father do, Alice?" the teacher asked.

"Sometimes he watches the football game on television," Alice said, "but mostly all he does is take out the garbage."

435, 592.

OFFICE

529. The man appeared to be half asleep at the breakfast table and in no hurry to rush off to work. "I think I'll have another cup of that delicious coffee," he mumbled, still not fully awake and aware of his surroundings.

"Here's your coffee," his wife said. "I hope it wakes you up because if you don't hurry you are going to be late to the office."

"Office! Office!" he shouted. "I thought I was already there."

OPERATION

530. A surgeon was making his hospital rounds and was chatting with a young lady he had operated on a few days earlier.

"Do you think the scar will show?" she asked the doctor.

"That will be entirely up to you," he said.

212, 779.

OPINION

531. "How did your date go last night, Dave?"

"Great. We got along fine. I told her a lot of my funny stories. She said she thought I was a real wit."

"Well, she was certainly half right."

532. Two women were chatting. "Do you know what Helen said about you?" the first asked.

"I haven't an idea in the world," her friend said.

"Yes," the first woman said, "that's exactly what she said—word for word."

533. A deputy sheriff had arrested a man for car theft. When his fingerprints were run through the computer, it was found that he was wanted by the FBI on a Federal charge. After the Federal agents had picked up the prisoner, the deputy had to fill in the usual report forms. After giving the prisoner's name, his many aliases, and other information about him, the deputy came to this question, "Disposition of the prisoner."

Being thorough and conscientious, he gave the question much thought and then wrote, "Mean and surly."

55, 78, 84, 96, 100, 182, 257, 318, 426, 463, 507, 701, 703, 706.

OPPORTUNITY

534. A woman's aunt, just past 80, had agreed to go to a rest home, but only on a two-week trial basis. When the niece took her there, she packed a small overnight bag for her aunt with a few bare necessities.

Two days later, the niece received a phone call from her aunt. "Please bring me some more clothes. I want that new pink print dress and that flowered overblouse, and be sure to bring my black beaded cocktail dress. And if you don't mind, I'd like to borrow your new blonde wig. I'm going to like it here. You didn't tell me, but there are men in the place."

439, 474, 567, 632.

OPTOMETRIST

535. An optometrist was instructing a new employee on how to charge a customer.

"As you are fitting his glasses and he asks how much they will cost, you say, 'Twenty-two dollars.' Then, you hesitate for just a few seconds and watch his eyes carefully. If his eyes don't flutter, you then say, 'For the frames. The lenses will be fifteen dollars.' Again, you pause and look into his eyes. If they still don't flutter, you say, 'Each.' "

ORCHESTRA

536. The community orchestra had been planning and rehearsing for their annual concert for nearly five months.

At the final dress rehearsal the night before the big event, the conductor took time during a rest period to thank everyone who had helped over the months. He thanked the sponsors, the members of the press, the ladies who had helped with the costumes and everyone else he could think of. Finally he said, "I want to pay a special tribute to the one person who hasn't missed a single rehearsal. Everyone else has missed at least one night except Joe Harrison, our first violinist. I'd like him to stand and be recognized. And maybe he would like to say a word."

The applaude was deafening. When it had quieted down enought for Joe to speak, this is what he said, "Thank you very much. I thought it was the least I could do since I won't be here tomorrow night for the concert."

OUTDOORS

537. Two women where chatting when the telephone truck drove up in front of one of their homes.

"Are you having trouble with your telephone?" her friend asked.

"No," she said. "we're having a 50 foot extension put on the telephone because we want our teenager daughter to spend more time outside now that Spring has come and the weather is so nice."

PAIN

538. A man thought he was going to die with a toothache. He asked his friend, "What can I do to relieve my suffering?"

"I'll tell you what I do," his friend said. "When I have a toothache, or any other kind of pain for that matter, I go over to my wife and she puts her arms around me and caresses me and soothes me until finally I forget all about the pain."

His friend brightened up and said, "Gee, that sounds like a wonderful idea. Is she home now?"

375.

PANHANDLER

539. The panhandler stopped a man on the street and asked for money for a cup of coffee.

"I don't hand out money on the street," the man said.

"What do you want me to do," the panhandler asked, "open an office?"

540. The panhandler stopped a man on the street and asked him for a dime for a cup of coffee.

"I'll give you a dime on one condition," the man said, "that you'll take me with you. I want to find the place that still sells a cup of coffee for a dime."

541. A woman answered a knock on her back door and saw a beggar standing there. "Lady," he said, "I'm hungry. I haven't eaten in two days. Could you give me something to eat?"

"I don't have much myself," she said, "but I'll be glad to share it with you. Do you mind eating some beef stew left over from the night before?"

"That would be fine," the beggar said.

"Okay, then," she said, "come back tomorrow."

542. When the housewife answered the doorbell, a tramp was standing there.

"Excuse me ma'am," he said, "would you please give me a drink of water, I'm so doggone hungry I don't know where I'm going to sleep tonight."

543. A panhandler stopped a man on the street and said, "Please give me enough money for dinner tonight. I have asked for, begged for and cried for money all day long. I'm hungry."

The man said to the panhandler, "Have you ever tried work?"

"Not yet," the panhandler said. "I'm going through the alphabet and I haven't come to W yet."

385, 825.

PARTNER

544. A man lay dying in the hospital. The doctors knew the man had only a few minutes left to live; so they had asked the family to leave the room. But the man insisted that he talk to his business partner. "I know I have only a few minutes to live," he said, "but I must say one final word to him."

So, the doctors let the partner in to see him. "I have something to confess to you," the dying man said. "For the past three years I have been stealing from the business and I want to say I'm sorry. I had to get it off my mind before I died. I wanted you to know."

"I already know," his partner said. "why do you think I poisoned you?"

PARTY

545. The cocktail party at the large country estate was a busy affair. More than 200 guests were milling around, drinking, eating hors d'oeuvres, chatting, getting acquainted and otherwise having a good time. At the height of the activities, a woman singled out the hostess and said, "Excuse me, but can you help me find that pretty little dark haired girl who was passing out the drinks a little while ago?"

"Oh," said the hostess helpfully, "are you looking for a drink?"

"No," the woman said. "I'm looking for my husband."

89, 340.

PATIENCE

546. A husband and wife were shopping in a supermarket. While the wife was filling her basket with groceries, the husband was at the other end of the store pushing the baby cart.

Much to his distress, the baby was howling and screaming with a temper tantrum.

"Take it easy, Willy," the husband said, "don't get upset. We'll soon be out of here and back home. Everything will be all right, Willy, if you just take it easy. Now, now, Willy, don't boil over where everybody can see you. Take it easy. Take it easy."

At last the shopping was over and mother and father and the baby were together at the checkout counter. Mother had picked up the baby and had put an all day sucker in his mouth and had quieted him down. A kindly grandmother type who had witnessed the whole episode said to the lady, "I certainly did admire the patience your husband showed while he was trying to comfort little Willy."

"Willy?" the mother said. "The baby's name is George. Willy is my husband."

547. A small boy was standing at the foot of a down escalator in a large department store. He was staring intently at the moving handrail.

The floor manager walked up to him and said, "Is there something wrong, little fellow?"

"No," the little boy said, "I was just waiting for my bubble gum to come back."

179, 369, 458, 553, 599.

PATROLMAN

548. The patrolman had stopped a driver late at night. The man knew he had not been speeding; so he asked the patrolman, "What did I do wrong?"

"You are driving without a rear light," the officer said.

The man got out of his car to look and suddenly began to go to pieces. "Oh, oh, oh," he cried. "This is terrible. My, I don't know what I'm going to do. How in the world did this happen without me knowing it?"

"Calm down," the officer said, "It isn't all that bad. Not having a rear light isn't that serious."

"Rear light?" the man screamed. "I don't care about the light. What about my boat and trailer?"

549. A lady had run a stop sign, and the patrolman drove up beside her with his light flashing and said, "I'm sorry, lady, but you'll have to pull over to the side of the road."

He then proceeded to give her a traffic citation.

Later, when she had paid her fine, she was afraid to let her husband find out what had happened. So, she marked the stub in her check book, "One pull-over, $35.00."

550. A car speeding down the Interstate was spotted by a flying patrolman. He radioed his partner on the ground and the patrolman in the car stopped the speeder and began writing a citation. "How in the world did you know I was speeding?" the man asked.

The patrolman didn't say anything, but pointed skyward.

"Do you mean to tell me that he's turned against me, too?" the man moaned.

551. The driver brought his car to a careful stop in front of the building marked "State Highway Patrol." Almost instantly, a patrolman carrying a clipboard opened the right hand door and slipped into the seat beside the driver.

"Let's go," the patrolman said. "Ease the car into traffic and go straight ahead." Once in the stream of traffic, he went through the usual safety checks; turn right, turn left, park it, back it up, test the brakes and the turn indicators and the horn.

At that point the driver turned to the patrolman and said, "Excuse me, but what is this all about? I'm on my vacation and just stopped at the Highway Patrol office to get a road map."

243, 245, 418, 484, 764, 765, 768.

PERFECTION

552. Someone asked the distinguished speaker what he considered an ideal audience.

"The ideal audience," he said, "is one that is highly intelligent, well educated—and just a little bit drunk."

279, 732.

PERSISTENCE

553. On a windy day in the Spring, a snail was slowly working his way up the side of the mulberry tree. Thinking they would have some fun teasing him, a couple of robins started to heckle him. "Hey," one of the robins said, "don't you know there aren't any mulberries in that tree this time of year?"

"That's right," the snail said, "but there will be by the time I get there."

554. The newspaperman was interviewing the old man on his 100th birthday. "To what do you attribute your longevity?" the newspaperman asked.

"Well, now, young fellow," the old man said, "you might call me a health nut. I never smoked, I never drank, I was always in bed and sound asleep by 10 o'clock every night. Besides that, I always walked three miles every day—rain or shine."

"But," said the newspaperman, "I had an uncle who followed that exact routine and he died when he was 62. How do you account for that?"

"All I can say is that he didn't keep it up long enough," the old man explained.

138, 474, 613.

PERSONALITY

555. Two young ladies were chatting. "How are things going with your new boyfriend?" the first one asked.

"Oh, I dropped him already," her friend said. "By the time we had our second date I discovered he had a split personality. And I also discovered that I couldn't stand either one of them."

556. A young lady visited her psychiatrist to get help for nervous tension and stress and strain. "I'm irritable most of the time, and it's hard for me to get along with people," she said.

The psychiatrist talked to her at some length about her problem and then prescribed a tranquilizer for her to take for her nervous tension.

Two weeks later when she returned for a second talk with him, he said to her, "Have you noticed any difference in your condition?"

"Not that I can notice," she said, "but I notice that everybody else has calmed down and that they have been much nicer than before."

PERSUASION

557. A young man was visiting his girlfriend. As they sat in her living room they were being pestered by her younger brother, who wanted to watch television.

Finally, the young man said to the kid, "Hey, here's a quarter, how about going down to the supermarket and having yourself a Coke?"

"Okay," the kid said, "but I hate to go alone. What about my friend next door?"

"Okay," the young man said, "here's another quarter, get two Cokes."

"What about his sister?" the kid asked. "She'll make trouble if we don't take her along."

"Okay," the young man said. "Here's another quarter, get three Cokes."

The kid said thanks and hurried to pick up his friends and take them to the supermarket.

The moral of this story is simple. You can get kids to do anything you want if you coax them enough.

136, 485.

PHARMACIST

558. A little old lady regarded the youthful looking pharmacist doubtfully. "I take it for granted," she said, "that you are a qualified pharmacist?"

"Oh, yes, ma'am," he said.

"You have passed all the required examinations?" she asked.

"Yes, ma'am," he said again.

"You've never poisoned anybody by mistake, have you?" the lady asked.

"Why, no!" he said.

"In that case," she said. "please give me a box of epsom salts."

631.

PHOTOGRAPHER

559. The city editor was breaking in a young man who had just been added to the photographic staff of the newspaper.

"This is the first day of Spring," he said to the rookie photographer. "How about going out to the zoo and getting some animal pictures?"

"That sounds like a good assignment," the rookie said. "What sort of pictures did you have in mind."

"Oh," the editor said, "use your own imagination. You can always find some interesting shots at the monkey cage."

The rookie spent all day at the zoo and finally returned to the office without having taken a single picture.

"What!" shouted the editor. "Surely you could have found something to photograph. Why didn't you go to the monkey cage like I told you?"

"I did," the rookie said. "I stood there all afternoon watching them, but I couldn't take their pictures because they never did shake hands with each other."

560. The wealthy society matron was looking at her new photograph that she had just had made. "That picture is terrible," she said to the photographer. "Now, I ask you, does that look like me?"

The photographer, who should have been a politician or at least a member of the Diplomatic Corps, smiled and said without batting an eye, "Madam, the answer to that question is in the negative."

PLANNING

561. The professor was forced to look for an apartment because the building he was living in was being torn down to make way for a parking lot. Apartments were almost impossible to find, and he was at his wits' ends to locate a place to live.

At last he had a brilliant idea. He went to a large apartment that was filled and asked the manager if he could see the list of tenants. As he and the manager ran down the list together, the professor said, "There, that one. I'll take it the first of the month. That's a student of mine. I know it will be vacant because I suddenly have a feeling that he is going to flunk physics and chemistry and get sent home."

334.

PLUMBER

562. A lawyer called a plumber to fix a leaky faucet. The plumber eventually arrived, and after about ten minutes of work the faucet had stopped dripping.

"How much do I owe you?" the lawyer asked.

"Counting mileage and parts and time," the plumber said, "that will be $18.00."

"What!" shouted the lawyer. "That's outrageous. Eighteen dollars for ten minutes of work. I'm a lawyer, and I don't make that kind of money."

"Neither did I," said the plumber, "when I was practicing law."

156, 631.

POLICE

563. A female voice on the phone at three A.M. begged the police to come as fast as they could. She said her husband was awakened by a noise in the back yard and when he went outside to investigate he was set upon and struck down by an unseen attacker.

A patrolman was dispatched from the police station at once and he was on the scene of the crime within minutes. Half an hour later he returned to headquarters with a sour look on his face and a huge lump on his forehead.

"Back already?" the desk sergeant asked. "Did you find the attacker?"

"Yes," the patrolman said, "I stepped on the rake, too."

4, 46, 766.

POLISH STORIES

564. A speaker had been regaling his audience with Polish stories. After his speech, Pete Petrowski said to him, "I was fascinated with all of your Polish jokes. I wondered where you found all of them. Do you by any chance read Polish?"

"No, I don't," the speaker said.

"Then, do you speak Polish?" Petrowski asked.

"No, I don't speak it, either," the speaker said.

"Well, tell me then," Petrowski said, "how does it feel to be stupider than one of us dumb Polacks?"

POLITICIAN

565. The candidate for Congress had been haranguing the crowd for more than an hour. As he came toward the end of his speech, he said, "Before I leave, does anyone have a question?"

"Yes," shouted a man from the rear. "Who else is running?"

566. "I see by the paper," a man said to a friend, "that they have indicted him for taking a bribe. The story says he was arrested as he was trying to flee the country. I guess that will be the end of his career."

"Yes," said his friend, "it looks like it. You might say he ran for mayor and made it, he ran for the state legislature and made it, he ran for Congress and made it and he ran for the border and didn't make it."

567. After a hard campaign for Governor, the politician sat in his campaign headquarters watching the results on television. When it became obvious that he had lost, a young and pretty little newspaper woman came up to him with her notebook and pencil in hand and asked, "What are your plans, now?"

"I appreciate you asking me," he said. "I don't have anything planned. What are you doing this evening?"

568. The candidate was beating the bushes for votes and stopped to talk to a farmer working in his garden.

"Here's my card," he said. "I'm running for the state legislature and I hope you'll vote for me."

"Vote for you?" the man shouted. "Why, I'd rather vote for the Devil himself."

"Well," the candidate said, "in case your friend decides not to run, I'd like you to vote for me."

569. A woman was helping in her husband's campaign for governor by handing out literature in front of the post office. As she asked one woman to vote for her husband, she was told, "I wouldn't vote for him if he was the last man running. He is a terrible man."

The candidate's wife was unperturbed and said, "I think that if you would read this brochure about him, you might find something about him that you would like."

As the woman glanced at the brochure, she saw a picture of the candidate with his wife and she immediately realized whom she was talking to. For a moment she was terribly embarrassed and was at a loss for words. But she soon recovered her composure and said, "I really didn't mean any harm. Frankly, if you knew my husband, you wouldn't like him either."

570. A politician and his wife were having dinner at a fashionable restaurant. Since he was well known, a great many people stopped at their table and shook hands and spoke. Each time, the politician would tell his friends about his recent fishing trip.

After a while his wife whispered to him, "I think it's nice that so many people stop to speak to you. And I see nothing wrong with you telling them about your fishing trip. But, each time you tell about the fish you caught, you change the size of the fish and the number. Why in the world do you do that?"

"Well," he said to his wife, "I know all of those people. They are voters and I want them to trust me and take me at my word. So, I make it a practice never to tell them more than I think they will believe."

85, 103, 114, 118, 168, 169, 174, 262, 361, 573, 708, 720, 748, 803.

POLITICS

571. A Congressman was being interviewed by the press. One reporter asked him, "Do you feel that you have influenced public opinion, sir?"

"No," answered the Congressman. "Public opinion is something like a mule I once owned. In order to keep up the appearance of being the driver, I had to watch the way he was going and then I followed as closely as I could."

572. The pollster was questioning the housewife about her voting preferences in the upcoming election.

"Oh," she said. "I never vote. I don't want to feel in any way responsible for what goes on in Washington."

117, 810.

POPULARITY

573. The man's campaign for office had been in full swing for about three weeks when a friend asked him, "Well, how do things look? Have you taken a poll of any kind?"

"Yes, I have," the candidate said. "The results came in yesterday. My first sampling shows that I am ahead seven to five. Next week I'm going to take another poll—this time, outside of my immediate family."

POWER

574. The corporation was family owned. Although the majority of the stock was owned by the widow of the founder she left the management of the company to her three sons and half a dozen grandchildren. During one of her rare visits to a Board of Directors meeting, a long argument had taken place regarding a new product that the company was planning to introduce.

After the discussion had reached the point of repetition and boredom, the little old lady spoke up and said, "I have a suggestion. Please understand that this is only a suggestion, but also remember who is making it."

PRAYER

575. A church deacon had done a bit of backsliding and had come home drunk the night before. Now, he was lying in bed suffering from an excruciating hangover.

His wife had tiptoed into the room and was trying to comfort him. "I think it would help if I said a prayer for you," she said.

He didn't say anything, so she began, "Lord, please help my husband. He is a good man. He feels so sick this morning because last night . . . ."

At that point, the sick man opened his eyes and touched his wife on the hand. "Honey, please don't tell him I got drunk. Tell him I have the flu."

576. A salesman who had been working in the New England area was being transferred to California. The move had been the principal topic of conversation around the house for weeks. Then, the night before the big move, when his five year old daughter was saying her prayers, she said, "And now, God, I'll have to say goodbye forever because tomorrow we are moving to California."

389, 577, 578.

PREACHER

577. A small-town minister received a call from a large, big city church. He was torn between going to the better paying job or staying with the local congregation. He said that before he made up his mind, he would give the problem a lot of prayer.

A week later, someone asked his six year old daughter if her father had decided what they were going to do.

"I'm not sure," she said, "My father is still praying and my mother is packing."

578. Church was over and the lady was backing out of the parking lot when she discovered she didn't have her handbag. She quickly parked her car again and rushed back to the pew where she had been sitting. Sure enough, her handbag was gone. As she stood there trying to think what to do, the minister walked up to her and said, "I'm sure you are looking for your handbag. Here it is. I saw it there and thought I had better pick it up for safe keeping."

"Oh, thank you," the woman said. "But surely no one would steal my handbag in church."

"No, I don't suppose so," the minister said, "But knowing my congregation as well as I do, someone might have seen it and considered it an answer to a prayer."

579. A minister had married his beautiful choir director and they were on their honeymoon. As they were driving down the road, he said to her, "My big problem now, darling, is to find someone to take your place. We will have to hire a new choir director."

"That will be easy," his bride said. "I have a person in mind. My cousin graduates next week from the conservatory of music."

"Wonderful," said her husband. "what is her name?"

"*His* name," said the clever bride, "is Bill Wilson."

580. The man's wife had taken to bed with a touch of the flu, so on Sunday morning he had to attend church without her. When he returned home after the service she asked, "What did the minister preach about?"

"Sin," her husband said.

"What did he say about it?" she asked.

"He was against it," the man said.

505.

PREJUDICE

581. Two secretaries were chatting over lunch. "How do you like your new boss," the first asked.

"He's all right, I guess," said her friend. "But, I find that he's very prejudiced."

"You mean over race and women's lib and all that?" the first secretary asked.

"Oh, no, nothing like that," her friend said. "He just thinks there's only one way to spell a word."

PRESIDENT

582. The teacher asked one of her students, "Do you know Lincoln's 'Gettysburg Address'?"

"No, I don't," he said. "But all of our other presidents have lived at 1600 Pennsylvania Avenue in Washington, D.C."

391.

PRIEST

583. A priest ran out of gasoline about six blocks from a filling station, and he walked there for a can of gasoline. The filling station manager was embarrassed because he didn't have a gasoline can. "Two people have walked off with cans in the past week," he said. "But, we'll figure out something."

He did. He came up with the idea of filling a dozen empty cold drink cans with gasoline and putting them in two six pack cartons. With one six pack in each hand, the priest walked back to his car and proceeded to pour the gasoline into his tank.

Just at that time, a Methodist minister, who was a friend of his, drove by. When he recognized his friend, he backed up to see if he could be of help. As he watched the priest empty the cold drink cans into his tank he said, "I must admit one thing. You Catholics sure do have more faith than we Methodists."

PRINCIPAL

584. One high scool student to another: "How about a little contribution? We're trying to raise some money for a going-away present for the principal."

"Oh, boy," said the other student, "is he leaving?"

"Not that we know of," said the first boy, "but we thought it was worth a try."

585. "Well," said a mother to her little girl, "what did you do at school today?"

"Nothing much," the little girl said, "Except our principal is leaving, so we all gave a donation to give him a little momentum."

502.

PRINCIPLE

586. A man had been invited to a rather large dinner party. As the pre-dinner drinks were passed around, he discovered that only fruit juice and punch were being served.

Then, when dinner was announced, he calmly picked up his hat and coat and headed for the front door. "You're not leaving, are you?" his host asked. "You were invited for dinner."

"I know," the man said, "but I never eat on an empty stomach."

PRISON

587. The convict had returned to prison, and the warden was questioning him. "I thought you were going to turn over a new leaf," he said. "I helped you get out on parole, and now a month later you are back. Why did you do it? Why are you back?"

"I'm here on account of my belief," the convict said.

"What do you mean, your belief?"

"Well," said the convict, "I believed the burglar alarm in the jewelry store had been disconnected."

588. A judge had just sentenced a 40 year old man to serve three 20 year terms in jail for armed robbery, attempted murder, and aggravated assault, to be served consecutively.

"But, Judge," the man said, "I can't serve those terms. I won't even live that long."

"Well," the judge said, "under the circumstances, why don't you just do the best you can?"

589. A woman who lived in the Kentucky mountains stopped by to chat with her neighbor. She found her in the midst of a major housecleaning. Her friend had washed and scrubbed the living room and was hanging new curtains.

"My," the visitor said. "You are fixing things up prettier than I ever saw. Are you planning to have a party?"

"No," her friend said, "it's more important than that. My son is coming home from prison tomorrow and I want everything to be real nice for him."

"I'm so glad to hear that," her friend said. "But I thought he had been sentenced for seven years for bootlegging. And he's only been gone two years."

"That's why we are so happy," the first woman said. "He is getting out five years early because of good behavior."

"That's wonderful," her friend said. "I know you must be proud to have such a good son."

746.

PRISONER

590. A big time gangster had escaped from the State penitentiary. This was big news, and almost at once the radio and television reports were telling the whole world about it. That was the news story of the hour.

About six hours after his escape, the gangster returned to the prison and turned himself in to the warden.

"Why did you come back?" the warden asked.

"Well," said the gangster, "it was like this. About four hours after I had escaped, I managed to make my way home. As I walked up the sidewalk to my front door, my wife was standing there screaming, 'You bum. You escaped four hours ago. Where have you been?' "

591. The judge was furious with the deputy sheriff in charge of the prisoner. "I understand that when court was over, he escaped," the judge shouted. "Why didn't you have all of the exits guarded?"

"I did," said the deputy, "but he walked out through the entrance."

533.

PROFESSION

592. Two friends who hadn't seen each other in years met in a supermarket and brought each other up to date on their families.

One lady said, "And tell me, Mrs. Wilson, how is your son, George?"

"He's getting along fine," she said. "He is a poet. He just received his master's degree in literature from the university."

"And what about Ethyl?" the first asked.

"She's just as smart as George," her friend said. "She graduated last year from college with a degree in modern art."

"Oh, yes," the first lady said. "and how is little Willy? What is he doing?"

"Well," her friend said, "Willy is still Willy. He wouldn't go to college. He said he likes to work with his hands. He became a plumber. And I want to tell you this. If it weren't for Willy, we'd all be starving to death."

368.

PROFESSOR

593. A young lady had graduated from college and decided to stay in school and work toward her master's degree. She received a work grant and was assigned as an assistant to the philosophy professor who had taught her the year before. She was delighted to be working with him, and everything went well until she was asked to type up the final examination questions. As she began to type them she realized that they were exactly the same questions that had been given to the students the year before.

"Is this correct?" she asked the professor. "Are you giving the same questions? Don't you know the students will get on to that and pass them on from year to year?"

"Oh, that's all right," the professor said. "It's true that I never change the questions. All I do is change the answers."

400, 447, 561.

PROGRESS

594. The patient with a stomach disorder was making a return visit to his doctor about it. After his consultation, the doctor said, "Have this prescription filled and take the medicine as directed. Also, I would suggest that you eat a good meal before going to bed at night."

"But," the man said, "the last time I was in here, you told me not to eat anything before going to bed."

Not to be caught in a mistake, the doctor said, "That just goes to show you how rapidly medical science has progressed since you were here."

PROTECTION

595. The race for sheriff had been hot and heavy, but the final count was absolutely one-sided: 3,400 votes for the winner, 102 votes for the loser.

The morning following the election, the loser was seen striding down the main street of the county seat with a big revolver on his hip.

"What are you carrying a gun for?" someone asked him.

"Listen, buddy," the loser said, "anyone in this county who doesn't have any more friends than I have, had better carry a gun."

PSYCHIATRIST

596. A woman who suffered from tension and fits of temper visited her doctor. Among other things, he prescribed certain tranquilizers.

A week later a friend asked her, "Do you feel any better? Are the tranquilizers doing you any good?"

"I don't know for sure whether or not I like the idea," the woman said. "Yesterday I caught myself being nice to a woman I shouldn't even be speaking to."

597. A woman visited a psychiatrist. Her problem, she said, was shoplifting. She was a kleptomaniac. The doctor treated her, and after six months of weekly visits, he said to her one day, "You don't need to come back anymore. You are cured. No more shoplifting."

The woman expressed great appreciation for the doctor's help. But, as she was leaving his office, he said, "By the way, if you should have a relapse, how about picking up one of those new electric digital clocks for my desk?"

598. Two newspaper editors met just outside the door to a psychiatrist's office.

"Hello," said the first editor. "Imagine seeing you here. Are you coming or going?"

"If I knew that," the second editor said, "I wouldn't be here."

599. A man's uncle died and left him 500 acres of land in Texas. Just before his death, his uncle had signed an oil lease with a wild-cat driller. From that day on, that 500 acres of land and the oil lease became the main topic of conversation of the lucky heir. For three or four years, he talked about the oil that would be coming in on his property. It became an obsession. That was all he could talk about. His family felt that he might be losing his mind over it; so they persuaded him to visit a psychiatrist. After visiting the psychiatrist twice a week for three months, he had reached the point where he hardly ever mentioned his imaginary oil well. "I think we are approaching a cure," the psychiatrist told him one day. "I think about four or five more visits should put you in perfect shape."

But, after that, the man never returned. Several weeks later, the psychiatrist saw him on the street and said to him, "Why did you stop coming to me for treatment? You weren't quite cured. Another visit or two would have done it."

"Oh," the man said, "I didn't have to come back any more. They struck oil on my property in Texas just like I said they would."

600. A woman visited the psychiatrist for the first time. He invited her into his office and asked her to make herself comfortable on the couch. Seeing that she was hesitating and seemed to be bashful, he said, "Go ahead and lie back and get comfortable. This is the way I have all of my patients talk to me. This is an important part of your treatment."

The woman did as she was told. She carefully smoothed her dress around her knees and then reclined and began to relax.

"Now," the doctor said, "Let's begin at the beginning. How did your troubles begin?"

"Exactly like this," she said.

601. A marriage counselor was training his assistant and asked him to sit in on a rather serious problem between a man and his wife. The counselor listened to each of his clients separately.

After hearing the wife's side of their problem, he patted her on the hand and said, "You are so right. You are so right."

Then he listened to the husband's side of the argument. As the man was leaving, the psychiatrist patted him on the shoulder and said, "You are so right. You are so right."

When the couple had gone, the counselor's assistant said, "Hey, you told the wife she was right and then you told the man he was right. What about that? You know they both can't be right."

And the psychiatrist looked at his assistant and said, "You are so right. You are so right."

481, 556.

PUBLISHER

602. The president of an ink manufacturing company hired a new secretary because of her looks and not abilities. He figured anybody could handle the small amount of correspondence that he took care of personally. For example, on her first day as his secretary he dictated only one letter. It went to a publisher. As he finished dictating he said to her, "You can get the address of the company off of their letterhead."

He discovered his mistake the next day when the letter was returned from the post office marked insufficient address. The envelope read, "Prentice-Hall, Inc., Tokyo, London, Sydney, Toronto, New Delhi, Singapore, Englewood Cliffs."

54, 55, 656.

QUESTIONS

603. A woman had been called for jury duty, and the defense attorney was questioning her.

"What is your occupation?" he asked.

"Housewife," she said.

"What is your husband's occupation?" he asked.

"He's a manufacturer," she said.

"Children?" he asked.

"No," she said. "He manufactures sewer pipe."

188, 324, 364, 513, 593, 735, 810.

RACE

604. Two sports car fans were sitting and chatting about cars while watching a drag race. One of them was bragging about his brother.

"He's the greatest mechanic you ever saw," he said. "He made his own car. He used the wheels from a Ford, a radiator from a Chrysler, an engine from a Chevrolet, a transmission from a Continental and a body from a Buick."

"That sounds like a great car," his friend said. "With all of those parts from different cars, what did he finally end up with?"

"Five years," his friend said.

390.

RACE HORSE

605. As the auctioneers chanted their calls at the horse sale, a farmer watched a young city fellow bidding on an old broken-down Kentucky thoroughbred. The bidding was slow, and the young man succeeded in buying the horse.

The farmer couldn't help but wonder why the young man bought such a terrible horse. So he said to him, "Why in the world did you buy that horse?"

"I'm going to race him," the young man said.

The farmer looked at the young man and then at the horse and then at the young man again. "Well," he said, "if you do race him, you are sure to win."

606. As the horses were entering the paddock before the Kentucky Derby, the owner of one of the horses slipped him a small white pill when he thought no one was looking. But he was wrong. One of the track stewards saw him and rushed over and said, "I saw you. You were doping that horse. You're going to be disqualified."

"No," said the owner. "I just gave him a little sugar tablet. All horses like sugar. Sugar's not dope. Here, I'll show you." With that he took one of the little tablets and swallowed it. "Have one yourself," he invited the steward as he handed him one of the little pills.

The steward popped it in his mouth and said, "I guess you're right. It's nothing but sugar."

As the horses were being led onto the track, the owner whispered to his jockey. "Son, once they're off, keep your horse on the outside. Nothing in the world can catch him—except maybe me and the racing steward."

521.

RAILROAD

607. The meeting in the town hall had reached the red hot stage. Charges and countercharges were flying around the room when suddenly the front door opened and a man dressed in overalls stepped in. "A minibus is parked on the railroad tracks in front of the town hall," he shouted. "I'm the conductor and want to ask that it be moved."

"I so move," cried a voice in the back of the room.

"I second it," another voice said.

The chairman banged his gavel and said, "You've heard the motion. All in favor say aye."

"Aye," came the resounding cry.

"So ordered," the chairman said. "Now, let's get on with the other business that we were talking about."

RECOGNITION

608. As the stranger in town parked in front of the post office and got out of his car, a man he had never seen before rushed up to him and said, "Well, Bill Baker. I haven't seen you in years. You sure have changed. You've lost about 50 pounds. And I believe you're three or four inches shorter than you used to be. And besides your hair has turned grey."

The stranger looked at the man and said, "You've made a mistake. My name isn't Bill Baker. It's Wilbur Sims."

"Oh," the first man said, "and you've changed your name, too."

514.

RELATIONSHIP

609. A woman had been hired and was filling in the many employment forms. She came to the portion where she had to name her husband on her tax deduction form. Following his name was this question, "Relationship to you?" Without hesitation, she wrote, "Very, very, nice."

486.

RELIGION

610. Two young ladies were chatting about a friend. "She didn't marry her boyfriend," one said, "because of her religious beliefs. He was broke, and she worshipped money."

119.

REMEDY

611. The little hyperactive boy had made a nervous wreck out of his mother. In desperation she took him to a doctor who prescribed a mild tranquilizer for him. Noting the mother's extreme tension and nervousness, the doctor also prescribed a tranquilizer for her. As she was leaving the doctor's office, he said, "Follow the directions carefully, and I want to see you again in a month."

A month later the woman visited the doctor alone. "Well," the doctor said, "how is the little boy getting along?"

"Who cares?" the woman said.

612. "Good morning," a man said to his friend. "You told me you were going to see the doctor yesterday. How did you make out?"

"All right, I guess," the man said. "The doctor nearly found out what I had."

"What do you mean, he nearly found out what you had?"

"That's right," the man said. "I had $15.75 and he charged me $15.00 for the office call."

209, 210, 219, 292, 422.

REPAIRMAN

613. Mrs. Thompson called the electrical repair shop and said, "You promised to send someone out to the house yesterday to fix our doorbell, and no one ever showed up. When are you going to fix it?"

"Oh," said the manager, "I'm sure we sent a man to fix it." Then he called to his newest helper, "Billy, didn't you go out to Mrs. Thompson's house on a repair call?"

"Yes, sir," he said. "I went right away like you told me. But when I got there I rang the doorbell for 15 minutes and nobody came to the door; so I figured there wasn't anybody at home and I came back to the shop."

REPUTATION

614. Two men who boarded an airplane in Washington, D.C. to fly to the West Coast were seated next to each other. To pass the time on the trip, they got acquainted and began to chat.

"I have just been released from the Federal Penitentiary at Lewisburg," the first man said, "and it's going to be very difficult to face all of my old friends back home."

"I know exactly how you feel," the other man said. "I am a member of Congress going back to my home town for two weeks during the Spring recess."

615. A wealthy businessman whose wife had died fell in love with a secretary who was 20 years younger than he was. For several months he showered attention on her. Night after night, he took her dancing and to the theater and to night clubs. He finally decided to ask her to marry him, but having learned caution in his years of business, he hired a detective agency to check up on her past. Several weeks later, when they reported to him, they said she had absolutely no scandal or misbehavior in her past. "However," the report said, "she has recently been seen enjoying the city's night life with an elderly man of rather questionable reputation."

79, 143, 237, 267, 333, 342, 388, 430, 478, 510.

RESTAURANT

616. As the man and his wife were leaving the restaurant after dinner, the proprietor was standing at the cashier's desk.

"How was your dinner tonight?" the proprietor asked.

"One thing I can say for your restaurant," the man said. "You surely must have the cleanest kitchen of any restaurant in town."

"Cleanest kitchen?" the proprietor asked. "You didn't go into the kitchen. How did you find out that it was so clean?"

"Because," the man said, "everything tasted like soap."

617. A man stopped in a restaurant, and the alert waitress brought him a cup of coffee immediately. Trying to be pleasant and start a conversation, he said, "Looks a bit like rain, doesn't it?"

"I guess maybe it does when you come to think about," she said, "but it's still coffee."

618. A clever restaurant owner had built a chain of some 30 quick food outlets that employed more than 600 persons. He was the perfect example of a man who was completely wrapped up in his work. He thought of little else.

The time came for his wife to go to the hospital to have her third child and he was in the waiting room along with half a dozen other expectant fathers. But, unlike them, he was not pacing up and down and chain-smoking cigarettes. He had found a small table in one corner of the room and had spread out a stack of papers and had gone to work just as though he were back in his office.

As he was totally absorbed in his figures and unaware of his surroundings, a nurse tapped him on the shoulder and said, "Excuse me, sir, it's a boy."

"Fine," the man said without looking up from his work, "have him fill in the usual employment forms and start him as a dishwasher."

619. A man opened a roadside restaurant and planned to specialize in steaks. After much though he decided to call his restaurant "The Miracle Restaurant." At the edge of town he put up this huge sign, "Eat with us. Remember, if it's a good steak, it's always a miracle."

620. A truck driver was asked about the food at a certain truck stop along his busy route.

"The food is terrible there," he said. "The mashed potatoes are watery, the green beans are tasteless, the roast beef is tough, the apple crust is limp and leathery and the coffee tastes like dishwater. But worst of all, they serve such small portions."

621. A man and his wife were spending a two-week vacation at a swank hotel in Florida. Each morning they had breakfast in the main dining room and always sat at the same table served by the same waitress. The first morning they were there, the man asked for whole wheat toast with his breakfast, but the waitress brought him white toast instead. The next morning he reminded her about the mistake the day before and again he orded whole wheat toast. Again she brought him white toast. This went on for 13 days. He always ordered whole wheat and the waitress always brought him white. On the last day there, he felt the game was up. So when the waitress took his order, he said, ". . . and white toast."

With a look of surprise she said, "Oh. I thought you always ordered whole wheat toast."

622. A customer in a swank restaurant said to the waiter, "I notice that the ash trays on the tables are genuine Waterford Crystal. They are very beautiful, but why do you have water in the bottom of them? Is that to help extinguish cigarettes?"

"Partly that," the waiter said, "but mostly to keep customers from slipping them into their coat pockets."

623. A couple visited a famous Chinese Restaurant in San Francisco. They were waited on by a charming little oriental waitress dressed in native costume. The menu had so many fabulous dishes and combination dinners that the couple were unable to decide what to order. Finally, the man said to the waitress, "Why don't you surprise us. Bring us your favorite dinner."

Within a few minutes she returned with two bowls of chili with side dishes of enchiladas, refried beans and guacamole.

624. A man ordered a large pizza.

"Do you want me to cut it into six pieces or eight?" the waitress asked.

"Better make it six," the man said. "I don't think I can eat eight pieces."

625. When the waitress gave the man his coffee, he discovered that he had a knife and fork, but no spoon. Trying to call attention to the oversight in a friendly manner, he said to the waitress, "I'm afraid this coffee is too hot for me to stir with my finger."

"Oh, my, I'm sorry," she said as she rushed back to the kitchen.

Within moments she returned with a big smile and another cup of coffee and said, "Here we are. This cup isn't as hot."

626. The waitress handed the man a menu, and trying to be helpful she said, "I have beef spare ribs, calf brains, hog liver, beef tongue, and . . . ."

"Hold it," the customer said, interrupting her. "You've got your troubles; I've got mine. Why don't you skip the sad story and bring me a hamburger with french fries, a cup of coffee and a piece of apple pie?"

144, 313, 514, 540, 570, 774.

RETIREMENT

627. After years of gulping down a quick breakfast and rushing off to work, the business executive retired. At breakfast on the first day of his retirement, his wife placed his usual breakfast of "eggs over light" before him and began to butter his toast.

"Darling," he said, "I don't want to be critical, but I wonder if you would cook my eggs straight up from now on. I hate them cooked over light."

"Do you mean that you don't like your eggs over light?" she asked. "Why, I've been fixing them for you like that every day for 40 years. Why are you waiting until now to tell me?"

"I never had time before," he said.

113, 215.

REUNION

628. The man had just returned from his 40th class reunion and was chatting to a friend.

"How did it go?" his friend asked. "Did you see a lot of your old friends?"

"Things didn't go so well," the man said. "All of my former classmates were so old and fat and bald that none of them recognized me."

629. A rich alumnus was attending the 20th reunion of his class. All of his former professors had either retired or passed away, except one old fellow who was still on the job. The alumnus was chatting with him and said, "I have made a lot of money and I would like to do something for my alma mater. Tell me, what studies did I excel in?"

"As near as I can remember," the old professor said, "you slept through most of my classes."

"Thanks for the suggestion," the alumnus said. "I'll build the college a new dormitory."

467, 507, 608.

REVENGE

630. A woman stopped to have her portrait made by a sidewalk artist. She said to him, "You will notice that I don't wear any jewelry except for a wedding band. But, in this portrait I want you to paint me with diamond earrings, a diamond bracelet and a three-strand diamond necklace. Make it look as though I am wearing about $100,000 worth of jewelry."

"I can do that, lady," the artist said, "But if you don't own that kind of jewelry, why do you want me to show you wearing it?"

"Because I am getting a divorce," she said. "And I am going to send this portrait to that little hussy my husband is going to marry. When she sees all the jewelry he gave me, she'll make life miserable for him until she gets the same thing."

631. A doctor called in a prescription to a pharmacist. As soon as he had put down the phone, the pharmacist began to roar with laughter and clap his hands with glee.

"What in the world is going on?" his assistant asked.

"Ho, ho, ho!" the pharmacist cried. "Do you remember that plumber who repaired our sink three months ago and charged us that outrageous price? Well, he'll be by in a little while to pick up this prescription."

101.

REWARD

632. A rich tourist decided to stop in a small out of the way town. As he parked his car and began to unload it in front of the motel room, his pet beagle dashed out of the car and took off after a stray cat. In spite of much whistling and calling and horn blowing, the beagle did not return. After waiting all night and searching through the town all morning, the tourist decided to place an ad in the local weekly newspaper.

"You are too late for this week," the editor said when the man visited the newspaper office. "The paper has gone to press and we'll be rolling in another 10 or 15 minutes."

"I sure wish you could squeeze this ad in someplace," the man said. "This is a pedigreed dog and I'm offering a $200 reward for him."

"Write out the ad," the editor said. "If it is that important, we'll stop the presses and hold up the paper for another 15 minutes."

The man wrote the ad, paid for it, and headed back to his motel. Half way to his motel the thought occurred to him that he had not included the motel phone number in the ad. He rushed back to the newspaper expecting to see everyone rushing around like mad. Instead, there was no one there except the janitor. The presses were not running and there was no one in the editor's office.

"Where is everybody?" he asked the janitor. "I expected to see the presses running and everbody working."

"Oh," said the janitor, "they stopped the presses and everybody took off about five minutes ago. They're out looking for somebody's lost dog."

ROBBERY

633. When the supermarket manager came to work one morning, he found that burglars had broken in the store the night before and had rifled the safe. On the door of the safe was this short note: "This should teach you a lesson. *Lower your prices!* How do *you* like being robbed?"

634. A little 82 year old woman got off the bus late one night and started toward the senior citizens' home a block away. Half way down the street a young hoodlum stepped out of an alley, grabbed her at gun point and pulled her into the dark shadows where he demanded her money.

She had not lived to be 82 years old without gaining a lot of courage and the ability to think fast. She proved it when she said, "Why, young man, you ought to be ashamed of yourself. I have grandchildren older than you. You shouldn't be picking on a little old lady like me. You should have some ambition. You ought to be robbing one of those all-night convenience stores."

46.

ROMANCE

635. Two young ladies were talking about some of their friends.

"I think the romance between Jean and Robert is headed for the rocks. It turns out that neither of them are good enough for the other one."

"Where did you ever get that idea?" her friend asked.

"I've been talking to both families," the first one said.

636. "Why do you date a man who is 30 years older than you?" a woman asked her friend.

"Because we like each other's company," her friend said. "He says he likes mine, and I'm absolutely sure I like his. I think he calls it the First National Bank."

637. During the summer vacation, two young people met and fell in love, and the young man proposed. The young lady said she would marry him, but not, under any circumstances, until after he had saved $2,000. They never discussed money again until the beginning of the Christmas season, when she said to him, "How much have you saved toward our marriage?"

"Times have been a little difficult lately," he said, "and all I have managed to save so far has been $65."

"Well," she said, "things being like they are, I'd say that was close enough."

638. The lights were low and the hi-fi was playing soft, romantic music. The young man held his sweetheart in his arms and whispered, "Darling, I love you more than anything in the world. I would lay down my life for you. I need you. I can't do without you."

"Wait a minute," the girl said, as she pushed him away.

"What's the matter?" he said.

"Nothing's the matter," she said, "but I just don't want to get that serious."

"Who's getting serious?" he asked.

639. Two women were chatting about their husbands. "If your husband should die," the first one asked, "do you suppose there is another man in the world just like him?"

"I doubt it," her friend said, "but if there was one, it would just be my bad luck to meet him."

640. When the pretty girl of 25 announced that she was going to marry a man of 65, all of her friends were horrified.

"You know very well," a friend said, "that these May and December marriages don't work out. Look what December will find in May; youth, beauty, vivaciousness, the very breath of Spring. But what will May find in December?"

"Santa Claus," the bride-to-be said.

641. A young man met a beautiful girl at a party one Saturday night. He arranged to take her to the theater on the following Monday night. Then, he took her dancing on Friday night. Before the evening was over, he had proposed marriage.

"But," she said, "this is too sudden. I like you and we seem to get along well, but after all, we know nothing about each other."

"Oh, yes I do," he said. "For three years I've been working in the accounting department of the bank where your father keeps his money."

642. The young man not only was romantically inclined; he was of the old school who asked permission of the girl's father before proposing to his loved one.

After he had asked for permission, the old man said, "So, you want to marry my daughter. Do you think you can support a family?"

"Well," the young man said, "I've got a pretty good job. And I think I can. How many of you are there?"

643. Three girls were the best of friends as they went through school together. Later, two of them married, but the third was still single at the age of 25.

Her friends sometimes chided her for not being married. One day they were needling her a bit and said, "Really, didn't you ever have a boyfriend? Have you ever been kissed? Did any man ever ask you to marry him?"

A bit irked at her friends, she said, "You wouldn't believe me it I told you. Why don't you ask your husbands?"

644. "How did you finally get him to propose?" a young lady asked her friend.

"It took a bit of planning," her friend said, "but I found his weakness. I prepared a home cooked meal for him and served it in a bikini."

645. The Eskimo boy was trying to impress his girlfriend. "I mushed through more than 40 miles of snow to visit you tonight."

"That's a lot of mush," she said.

646. Two little boys were at the movies. One of them said to the other, "I must be growing up. These love scenes don't make me sick anymore."

34, 272, 320, 461, 462, 475, 527, 684, 714.

SALESMAN

647. A high powered entrepreneur had stopped in a bar for a drink and struck up a conversation with the man next to him.

"You look a little bit sad," he said, "What's your problem? Everybody has a problem."

"Yes," the man said, "I have a tiny problem. I promised my wife I'd get her a Pomeranian for her birthday, and the best price I can get on one is $185, and that's just too much."

"I'll say it is," the entrepreneur said. "You are getting ripped off. I'll sell you one for $110."

"Man, am I glad I ran into you," the man said. "How soon can you deliver it?"

"Let me make a phone call and I'll let you know," the entrepreneur said.

He went to the phone and called his partner. "Hey," he said, "I've just sold a fellow a Pomeranian for $110. He wants to know how soon we can make delivery. But, before we talk about that, tell me, what in the world is a Pomeranian?"

648. A young man called on the publisher of a weekly newspaper.

"Do you need an editor?" he asked.

"No," said the publisher, "we don't."

"Do you need an advertising man?" the salesman asked.

"No, I don't need one," the publisher said.

"Do you need a printer?" the salesman asked.

"No we don't," the publisher said. "The truth is we don't need anybody. We have all the help we can use."

"In that case," the salesman said, reaching into his sample case, "You will want one of these 'No Help Wanted' signs."

649. Two salesmen met on the elevator as they were leaving work for the day. "What sort of day did you have?" the first one asked.

"I had a great day," his friend said. "I established a lot of goodwill for the company all over town. How did you do?"

"I didn't sell anything either," his friend said.

650. The insurance salesman was trying to convince the young married man that he should provide for his wife in case of his untimely death.

"How would your wife carry on after you were gone," he asked, "if you should die suddenly in an accident?"

I don't know," the young man said, "and I'm not sure that I care just as long as she behaves herself while I'm still alive."

651. The life insurance salesman had tried his best to make the sale but couldn't get a commitment from the man. Finally, he stood up to leave and said, "I certainly don't want to frighten you into a decision. Please sleep on it tonight and if you wake up in the morning, let me know what you think about it."

652. A housewife who was slightly hard of hearing answered her doorbell to find a salesman standing there with a large sample case.

"Good morning," he said. "I represent the Amalgamated Woolen Mills. We are offering a special price on a large stock of woolen yarns that didn't come up to our proper standards when it was dyed. The colors ran and the yarns are a bit off color. I'd like to come in and show you my samples."

The woman hadn't understood him very well and said, "I'm sorry, what did you say?"

This time the salesman raised his voice and said, "Would you be interested in some off-color yarns?"

"I think it would be fun," the lady said. "Come on in and we'll have a cup of coffee while you tell them to me."

653. The man was several weeks behind with his yard work. Being somewhat of a psychologist, he decided to pull the old "Tom Sawyer" stunt on the kids in the neighborhood. He set up a lemonade stand in the yard and invited all of them to come over for the fun. He gave each of them a ride on his mower and then divided up the fun; the fun of raking the yard, of loading the plastic bags with leaves, of trimming the walks, of weeding the flower beds. He and the kids had great fun together. They sang songs and he had a few lollypops for prizes, and, all in all, he finagled those kids into doing a lot of work.

Early the next morning, the man's doorbell rang, and when his wife opened the door, there stood a cute little five year old girl who said, "Can he come out to play again today?"

654. The owner of a country store in the Tennessee mountains was invited to go into Knoxville to hear a famous sales manager talk about the art of selling. The speaker told the famous story about the young lady in the candy store who had more customers than the other clerks. "She noticed that when people ordered a pound of candy from the other girls," the great sales expert explained, "they would put more than a pound on the scales and then remove the candy piece by piece until they had exactly one pound. But this girl used psychology. She always put a little less than a pound on the scales and the. added candy piece by piece until she had a pound. The candy weighed the same, but oh, what a difference it made to the customer."

The owner of the country store took the lesson to heart, and when he returned to his store in the mountains he told his wife, "From now on when people order a dozen eggs, I want you to count them out, because the eggs will look larger in your little hands than in mine."

655. The sales manager was complaining to one of his salesmen about the way he sent in his reports. "They're terrible," the sales manager said. "Nobody can make heads or tails out of them. A good report should be written so that any numbskull can understand it."

"I agree with you," the salesman said. "Just what part of my report can't you understand?"

656. After a salesman for a large publishing company had spent four days at the American Booksellers Convention, he turned in his expense account. It was returned to him by the sales manager with this pencilled memo attached: "We certainly can't approve this expense account, but we would like to buy the fiction rights to it."

657. The book salesman was talking to a farmer. "Now that your boy has started school, you certainly should buy him an encyclopedia."

"Nope," the farmer said. "He can ride the school bus like the other kids. And if he misses it, then he can walk to school like I used to do."

658. A minister bought a used car which the salesman had insisted had "belonged to a little old-maid school teacher."

Three days later he drove back to the used car lot and said to the salesman, "I just came back to return some things the little old lady left in the glove compartment of her car; three packages of cigarettes and a half-pint of whiskey."

659. The small middle-class subdivision was pestered with door-to-door salesmen. Once they got a foot in the door, you could hardly get rid of them. Except for one housewife. Her neighbors noticed that the salesmen never went into her house. In fact, after about half a minute talking through the screen door, they always turned and walked away—rather rapidly.

Curious about what the woman was saying, a neighbor asked her about it.

"Oh, it's simple," she said. "Whenever a salesman comes to the door I say I'm glad he came. Then I invite him to come in and look over the new line of kitchen ware that I'm selling."

660. The busy sales manager was told by his secretary that four little Girl Scouts wanted to see him. "I think they are selling cookies," she said.

"Send them in," the sales manager said. "It will be interesting to see what sort of sales talk they use."

When the Girl Scouts had been ushered into his office, he said to them, "Good morning, young ladies. And just why did you want to see me this morning?"

"Because," said one of them, "everybody in town says you are so handsome."

After he had bought twelve boxes of cookies and the girls had left, the sales manager said to his secretary, "It's exactly what I've been preaching to my salesmen in our meetings—there is no better way than to be honest and stick to the truth."

72, 155, 185, 234, 405, 410, 411, 661, 789, 790, 797, 817.

SAVINGS

661. The home freezer salesman was trying to convince the housewife that she would save enough on her grocery bill to pay for the freezer.

"I suppose you are right," she said, "but we are paying on our washing machine with the money we save on our laundry; and we are buying a car on the bus fare we are saving; and a house on the rent we are saving. I'm afraid we just can't afford to save any more money right now."

56, 193, 417.

SCARCITY

662. Two old-maid sisters were spending their usual evening at home together when one of them looked up from the newspaper she was reading and said, "Listen to this. Here is a story about a woman who was married four times, and each time her husband died. And each time she had him cremated."

"That's the way life goes," her sister said. "Here we are sitting here without husbands and that woman had husbands to burn."

SCHOOL

663. The internationally known author was delivering the graduation address at the university. It was well written and was being delivered in a most inspiring manner. The theme was one of optimism and hope for the future.

Two foreign students were in the audience. One of them said to the other, who understood English, "What is he saying?"

"School is out," said the one who understood English.

664. A little girl came home from her first day at school. "What did you learn at school today?" her mother asked.

"Nothing much," the little girl said, "Because the teacher said I have to go back again tomorrow."

665. One student asked her friend, "Have you read any mysteries lately?"

"Yes," her friend said, "I'm reading one now."

"What's the title?"

"Advanced Algebra."

666. Two parents were chatting about their children. "How are your children doing in school this year?" the first one asked.

"Much, much better," her friend said. "But I still have to attend the PTA meetings under an assumed name."

667. The fourth grade teacher said, "Now, everybody, we're going to talk about Alaska and the Eskimos. I'm sure everyone has studied his lesson. So, Robbie, what do you know about the Eskimos?"

Robbie, who hadn't studied one word about the Eskimos, said, "They are famous for their delicious pies."

668. "Boy, this is great," a boy whispered to his fellow student. "We're not going to have that test after all."

"Sure we are," the other kid whispered. "The teacher said we'd have the test—rain or shine."

"Look out the window," the first student said with a grin. "It's snowing."

16, 79, 129, 300, 434, 452, 476, 502, 585, 710, 734.

SECRETARY

669. Two secretaries were chatting over lunch. "How do you like your new job?" the first one asked.

"Fine," her friend said. "And I'm sure they are going to keep me permanently."

"Oh," the first one said, "did they tell you that?"

"No," her friend said, "but yesterday the boss bought me a dictionary."

670. A man was in the midst of negotiating a highly confidential business deal. If the details leaked out, a multimillion dollar merger might fall through. So, he said to his secretary, "The papers in this brown envelope are dynamite—pure dynamite. I want you to file them carefully so that when I ask you for them I can have them immediately."

Being a conscientious worker, she marked the envelope "Dynamite" and filed it under the "D's."

671. Two secretaries were chatting about their work. "I hate filing," the first one said. "No matter how careful I am, I can't seem to find things. My problem is, I forget how I filed them."

"That's no problem with me," her friend said. "I just make 26 copies of every letter. Then I file one copy under each letter of the alphabet. Then, no matter where I look, there is a copy."

672. A businessman's secretary had slipped into the habit of arriving late for work several times each week. One Friday afternoon, just before quitting time, he called her into his office and said, "You are a very beautiful girl. I suspect I am the luckiest man in town to have such a pretty secretary. I am sure that men are constantly taking you to night clubs and out to dinner. I was just wondering, are you doing anything Sunday night?"

"At last," she thought. "Here is the opportunity I have been looking for. Finally, he has noticed me." So, she replied hopefully, "No, I don't have anything planned. What did you have in mind?"

"What I had in mind was this," he said. "Please go to bed early and get a good night's sleep so that you can be at work on time Monday morning."

12, 193, 269, 581, 602.

SENIOR CITIZEN

673. Two old-timers were chatting about things in general.

"The world isn't fair," the first one said. "When I was a kid, I was taught to respect old people and to listen to their opinions and advice. Now that I'm old, everybody tells me that I should listen to the young people."

674. Two old-timers were chatting about old friends as they played shuffleboard in Florida. "Of all my old friends who have passed away," the first man said, "I think I miss Willy Baker the most."

"Why do you miss him the most?" his friend asked.

"Because," said the first man, "I married his widow."

90, 113, 220, 288, 299, 360, 534, 554, 627.

SENTIMENT

675. A hold-up man had been caught and was being booked at the police station.

"Okay," the desk sergeant said, "take everything out of your pockets and put it on the desk. We'll put the things in a sealed envelope, and you can have them if and when you ever get out of jail."

One of the items placed on the desk was a well worn and shiny silver dollar.

"I wonder if I could keep that with me," the hold-up man said in a pleading tone. "That has great sentimental value for me. It's my lucky piece. You see, it's the first dollar I ever stole."

246.

SERVICE

676. The Sunday school teacher was teaching her kindergarten children about the Golden Rule. "Remember," she said, "we are here to help others."

"Then what are the others here for?" a little girl wanted to know.

SHIPPING

677. A woman returned home one Saturday afternoon from the beauty parlor to find her husband lying unconscious in the hallway. In his hand was a slip of paper, and by his side was a large cardboard box.

"Wonderful, wonderful!" she shouted. "My mink stole has come."

SHOPPING

678. "What?" the woman shopper said to the manager of the meat department. "Do you mean to tell me your turkeys are 69¢ a pound? They're on sale at the other supermarket for only 52¢ a pound."

The manager was a bit irked at the lady and said, "If you can buy turkeys so cheap over there, why don't you do it?"

"Because they are out of turkeys this morning—that's why," she said.

"Oh, I can do better than he can," the manager said. "Come back some day when I'm out of turkeys and I'll price them to you at only 39¢ a pound."

679. A woman returned home from a shopping spree loaded with packages. Her husband met her at the door and shouted, "What did you buy? With prices as high as they are, I'll bet you spent a fortune. I hate to think what has happened to our nest egg."

"I'll tell you what happened to it," his wife said as she began to put her packages on the dining room table. "The old hen got tired of sitting on it."

680. The supermarket was crowded. People were shoving and pushing each other all around, especially at the meat counter. Finally, the boss noticed one of the clerks arguing with a woman customer. Suddenly, she left in a huff.

"What was the matter?" the boss asked.

"Oh, she was complaining about the long wait," he said. "You just can't please that woman. Yesterday, she was complaining about the short weight."

681. A woman was shopping in the drug store and asked the clerk for a small tube of toothpaste. "I'm sorry," the clerk said. "We don't have the small size anymore."

"Well," said the customer, "I'll take a medium then."

"We don't have medium, either," the clerk said. "All we have are Large, Extra Large, Family Size and Jumbo."

682. A man visited a woman's dress shop and said to the clerk, "I'm looking for a birthday present for my wife."

"I'll be glad to help," the clerk said. "How about a pretty blouse? We have some on sale for only $19.00."

"Oh," said the man, "that is more than I wanted to pay."

"How about a bottle of perfume? We have some for $9.50," the clerk said.

"That's still more money than I had in mind," the man said.

"How about a pair of gloves for $6.95?" the clerk asked.

"That's still more than I want to pay," he said.

"Maybe a box of handkerchiefs for $2.00?"

"Still too high," he said.

Now the clerk was disgusted and said, "Why don't you send her a post card and write on it 'I LOVE YOU.' That will only cost you 11¢—if you can go that high."

683. A woman was standing in line waiting to be served at the local hardware store. She grasped her handbag with her left hand while her right hand was held closely against her waist with her thumb and forefinger stretched as far apart as possible. Another woman customer, seeing her standing in such an awkward and uncomfortable position, said to her, "My, you seem to have a terrible problem. What is it, arthritis?"

"Oh, no," the woman said cheerfully. "My husband is at home repairing our lawn mower and he needs a bolt this long."

684. A young couple was shopping for matching wedding rings. "I don't want one that is too wide or too tight," the young man said. "It might cut off my circulation."

"Hopefully, it's going to do that anyway," the young lady reminded him.

58, 72, 105, 127, 136, 164, 229, 261, 714.

SHOW BUSINESS

685. The medicine show at the county fair had attracted a large crowd, and the barker was in the midst of his spiel. "This bottle that I hold in my hand contains the elixir of life," he shouted. "It will restore your youth. It will keep you in perfect health. It will keep you from getting old. Look at me. Would you believe that I fought in the war of 1812? I'm over 200 years old."

A man standing near the front of the crowd spoke to the barker's youthful looking assistant, who was selling the elixir as fast as she could make change. "Is that man really 200 years old?" he asked. "Now tell me the truth."

"He claims to be," she said, "but I'm not sure. I've only been working for him for 120 years."

691.

SICKNESS

686. A man said to his friend, "I hear that your mother-in-law has been dangerously ill. How is she getting along?"

"Yes," said his friend, "she was dangerously ill and we took her to the hospital. But she is back now and dangerously well again."

SIGNS

687. The experienced womanizer spotted a beautiful girl standing alone at a cocktail party. Using one of the oldest gambits in the world, he walked up to her, introduced himself and said, "I'm a Leo. What is your sign?"

"No trespassing," she said with a cold stare.

155, 159.

SILENCE

688. A woman was complaining that she was coming down with the flu or a serious cold or something. So, her husband took her to the doctor.

Immediately, the doctor put a thermometer in her mouth. "Sit there quietly for five minutes," he said.

Of course, she did as she was told.

The husband was absolutely fascinated and said, "Doctor how much will you take for that thing?"

SLEEP

689. The bookkeeper was asleep at his desk when the boss came by. "Hey," the boss said, "wake up. Are you sick or something?"

"No," the bookkeeper said, "I guess I just dozed off. I didn't get a wink of sleep all night last night."

"That's terrible," his boss said. "Whenever I have insomnia, I imagine I'm watching sheep jumping over a fence, and then I start counting them, and I go right to sleep. It works every time. You should try that."

"I did," the bookkeeper said. "But somewhere near the beginning I made a mistake, and it took me all night to find it and get it straightened out."

690. A woman was chatting with her best friend. "After a busy week, do you ever wake up grumpy on Sunday morning?"

"No," said her friend, "that's the day I always let him sleep in."

691. A woman was complaining to a friend about her husband's snoring. "It's about to ruin my marriage and I don't know what to do about it," she said.

"That shouldn't bother you so much," her friend said. "My husband snores, too. I've learned to get used to it. I just turn my back on him and sleep with my ear as far away from him as I can get."

"That's what I have tried to do," the other woman sobbed. "But he's a ventriloquist and he snores on both sides of me."

30.

SMALL TOWN

692. A man had been invited to spend a week with a long-time friend who had moved to a mountain village in the Ozarks. He drove for miles down a deserted looking road and finally came to a country store at a crossroads. He asked the owner of the store how much farther it was to the little town he was looking for and he was told that he has passed it.

"I don't see how I could have passed it," he said. "I didn't see a store or a school or a filling station or a . . . ."

"That was it, that was it!" the man shouted.

SMOKING

693. An Air Force lieutenant checked into the dispensary with a hacking cough. "This cough is serious," the doctor said. "Do you smoke?"

"No," the lieutenant said. "I gave it up."

Unconvinced, the doctor said, "When did you give it up?"

"Nineteen fifty-nine," the lieutenant said.

Surprised, the doctor said, "That long ago? Impossible."

"I don't see why it's so impossible," the lieutenant said, looking at his watch. "It's only twenty-one sixteen now."

694. A man was shopping in an elegant department store that sold everything. In the tobacco department he bought a box of expensive cigars and opened it and started to light one up. The clerk pointed to a sign which said 'No smoking,' and said, "I'm sorry, sir, but we do not allow smoking in this store."

"What?" the man said in disgust. "Do you mean to say you'll sell me a box of cigars and yet you won't allow me to smoke one?"

"That's the way it is," the clerk said. "Remember, we also sell bath towels."

695. Two women were chatting at the supermarket.

"I haven't seen you in two weeks," the first woman said. "You were going to stop smoking the next day. Have you really quit?"

"So far," the second woman said, "I haven't had a cigarette."

"You'll remember I quit two years ago," the first woman said, "and it nearly drove me mad for the first three months. Has it bothered you?"

"It bothers me some," her friend said, "but when it does, I calm my nerves by kicking the dog, slamming the door and yelling at the kids."

92, 217, 376.

SNOW

696. A windshield scraper is a gadget that keeps falling out of your glove compartment all summer long, gets lost under the seat in the winter and snaps in two when you finally start to use it.

668.

SORRY

697. Just before boarding the plane, a couple was seen hugging and kissing and telling each other a sad and sorrowful farewell. At last the flight was called. The couple gave each other a final kiss and the woman sobbed quietly as she boarded the plane and took her seat. A grandmotherly type little lady had witnessed the whole affair and said to the woman. "I know exactly how you feel. You are unhappy because you must part for awhile from your husband."

"No, that's not it," the woman sobbed. "I'm crying because I'm on my way back to him."

SPEAKER

698. A speaker opened his remarks by saying, "My job is to speak to you today. As I see it, your job is to listen. If by any chance you should finish before I do, will you please raise your hand."

699. The banquet had been served, the desserts eaten and the final cup of coffee poured. The waitresses had left the dining room. The noise level was high in the room as the guests chatted and visited and joked with each other. Everyone was obviously having a good time.

The program chairman whispered to the guest speaker, "It looks like everybody is enjoying the evening. Do you think I should let them have a few more moments of fun or would you like me to introduce you now?"

700. The guest of honor had just been introduced and had made his opening remarks when the microphone fell off its stand. The program chairman jumped to the rescue at once and after a moment's adjusting and tightening of the bracket with his fingernail file, he said to the audience, "Don't worry. I'm sure it will be all right for the rest of the program. It's just that the speaker has a screw loose."

701. The banquet speaker had finished his address and the meeting had been dismissed. As the audience broke up and moved out of the dining room, a woman said to her husband, "Wasn't that an inspirational speaker?"

Her husband said, "Well, as far as I'm concerned, 30 minutes of rain would have done us a lot more good."

702. A noted speaker once was asked his secret of success.

"First," he said, "you write an attention getting opening for your speech—something that will attract everybody's attention. Then you write a dramatic summary and closing that will leave your audience spellbound. Then, you put them as close together as possible."

703. The annual Chamber of Commerce dinner was a gala affair. The men were dressed in their dinner jackets and the ladies were wearing their fanciest clothes. Jimmy Dunne was being installed as the new president, and the speaker for the evening was the State Senator for that district.

When the dinner was over and the people were leaving, Jimmy and his wife were standing at the door shaking hands with as many people as they could. As one lady was leaving, Jimmy's wife leaned over to her and said, "I don't think we've met. I'm Gladys Dunne."

And the lady said, "I'm glad he's done, too. That was the most boring speech I have ever had to sit through."

704. After the speaker had finished his address, the program chairman handed him a check.

"Oh," the speaker said, "I wouldn't think of accepting an honorarium from an organization that is devoted completely to community service. I was honored to be invited to speak to you today. Please donate the money to some worthy cause."

"Do you mind if we put it in our special fund?" the chairman said.

"Not at all," the speaker said. "What is the fund for?"

"So that we can get better speakers next year," the chairman said.

705. The congressman had a new administrative assistant and took him back to his district on one of his periodic speech making trips. The congressman's first speech was at a testimonial dinner put on by a group of his local supporters. When it came time for the main address, all the congressman did was tell jokes for 30 minutes. Not only that, but he told some of the oldest and most shop-worn jokes in the book. When the speech was over and the handshaking had finally worn itself out and the great man and his assistant were on their way back to their hotel, the assistant said, "Sir, you will excuse me for asking this, but why did you tell all of those lousy jokes this evening? In Washington, you are much more sophisticated. But tonight you told the oldest bunch of jokes I ever heard."

"Oh," the congressman said, "I did that on purpose. Those are supposed to be my unselfish supporters. So, as I was speaking, I watched every one of them carefully. You can be sure that those who laughed at those sorry jokes are the people who want something from me."

706. The audience was noisy and ill-mannered and was paying no attention as the main speaker was introduced. They continued to ignore him and make noise as he struggled with his opening remarks. After four or five minutes of complete frustration, he finally pounded on the lectern and shouted into the microphone, "Please, may I have a little quiet? You are making so much noise that I can hardly hear what I am saying myself."

At least one man in the back of the room was listening to him because he shouted, "Don't worry about it, mister, you aren't missing very much."

707. The luncheon speaker was obviously nervous as he struggled with his notes and the microphone and his glasses. "I hope you will forgive me for being a bit nervous," he said. "I must confess that this is only the second time I have ever spoken in public. The first time was in Louisiana some years ago when I proposed to my wife over a rural party line."

708. Two men were talking about a local politician. "Did you hear his last speech?" asked the first.

"I sure hope so," said the second.

709. Two men were listening to a politician who was campaigning for Congress.

"He sure uses a lot of big words, doesn't he?" one fellow said. "I don't know what he's talking about half the time."

"Oh," said his friend, "he uses those words because he knows that if everybody knew what he was talking about they would know he didn't know what he was talking about."

117, 240, 325, 552, 565, 663.

SPOILED BRAT

710. The five-year-old was spoiled rotten. His grandparents knew it. The neighbors knew it. But mother doted on him. He hardly left her side. And when he wanted anything, he either whined for it, cried for it, or threw a temper tantrum. Then came his first day away from her loving arms—his first day at school.

When he came home from school his mother met him at the door. "Was school all right?" she asked. "Did you get along all right? Did you cry?"

"Cry?" he asked. "No, I didn't cry, but the teacher did."

STATUS

711. A woman went to see her doctor and said, "I'd like to have an operation."

"An operation?" he said. "There's nothing the matter with you. What kind of an operation do you want?"

"Oh, it doesn't matter much," she said. "But when I go to cocktail parties and club meetings all the other women talk about their operations and I hate to be left out of the conversation."

252.

STRATEGY

712. A considerate husband who once offered to help his wife in the kitchen had been asked to wipe the dishes. After about three nights of helping her, he discovered he had become a victim of a work pattern that he couldn't get out of diplomatically. Night after night as he wiped dishes, he tried to think of some way to find relief. Then it dawned on him. On his wife's birthday, he bought her an expensive set of imported bone china. Now she won't let him touch them.

713. Three men were driving down a country road and came to a small town where a huge political-speaking and fish-fry was in progress. "Hey, that looks like a free meal," one of the men said. "Let's get in line."

They parked their car, got in line, and were fed a delicious meal. Just before the speaking was scheduled to begin the chairman stood before the microphone and said, "As you know, the fish fry is three dollars each. We didn't bother to have tickets printed so we're going to ask our campaign workers to go through the crowd and collect from each one of you."

Since the men didn't have that much money, they held a quick conference and solved their problem. One of the men fainted and the other two carried him to their car and drove off like mad.

714. The young lady had just returned from shopping for sport clothes to take on a summer cruise. She was showing her mother all the things she had bought.

"Look at this darling bikini," she said. "How do you like it?"

Her mother looked pleased and said, "One thing's for sure. If I had worn something like that when I was your age, you'd be four years older than you are now."

200, 235, 295, 383, 644, 659.

SUCCESS

715. The local used car dealer had just been named man of the year. At his big testimonial dinner he was asked by the TV newscaster, "To what do you owe your great success?"

"Five things contributed to my success," the man said. "First, I always treated others the way I wanted to be treated. Second, I always sold at a fair price. Third, I was always honest in my dealings. Fourth, I always treated my workers generously. Fifth, my aunt in Cleveland died and left me two million dollars."

386.

SUNDAY SCHOOL

716. The Sunday school teacher was teaching about the Ten Commandments.

"Can anyone tell me which Commandment has only four words?" she asked. "Now come on, the Commandment with only four words?"

"Keep off the grass," said the smart little boy on the front row.

717. Two little girls were talking about Sunday school. "Do you believe in the Devil?" one asked the other.

"Not really," the other little girl said. "It's just like Santa Claus. It's your father."

70.

SURPRISE

718. A man came home from work one day to find his house in a shambles. The beds hadn't been made, the kitchen sink was filled with dirty dishes, the children's clothes and toys and books were scattered throughout the house. Besides that, dinner wasn't ready.

"What in the world happened?" the man asked his wife when he saw the mess.

"Nothing," she said. "Absolutely nothing. You are always wondering what I do all day long. Well, take a look. Today, I didn't do it."

50.

SUSPICION

719. A man had arrived from a cross-country air flight and was met at the airport by his wife. As they were standing together at the baggage claim area an airline stewardess walked by with her overnight bag. The man spoke to her and said, "Thanks again for the nice flight from the West Coast, Miss Lewis."

"Who was that?" the man's wife asked.

"Oh, nobody in particular," the man said. "She was the stewardess on the flight I just came in on."

"So," said his wife, "you know her name. I'll bet you have her address and phone number, too."

The man was ready with his answer. "It's not that way at all. On each flight the names of the stewardess and the pilot and the co-pilot are posted on little plastic name plates in the front of the cabin. Everybody on board can see them. Besides, they announce their names before we take off."

"Okay, wise guy," his angry wife said. "If you are so smart, tell me the names of the pilot and co-pilot."

TALK

720. Speaking of his opponent, the politician said, "He reminds me of a fog horn. He repeatedly calls attention to the problem, but he never does anything about it."

355, 816.

TAXES

721. A visitor from Holland was chatting with his American friend and was jokingly explaining about the red, white and blue in the Netherlands flag. "Our flag symbolizes our taxes," he said. "We get red when we talk about them, white when we get our tax bill and blue after we pay them."

"That's the same with us," the American said, "only we see stars, too."

199.

TAXI

722. As the crowd was leaving the theater, two men rushed for the same taxi. After a brief discussion, one man shook hands with the other and let him enter the cab and drive away. When the loser returned to the curb and joined his wife, she said, "Why did you let him have the cab without so much as an argument?"

"Well," he said, "we talked about it and I figured he needed it more than I did. You see, he was late for his karate class."

723. Because it was pouring rain, the housewife decided to call a taxi to take her to the supermarket. The taxi firm that she called had a fleet of radio alerted cabs. As luck would have it, one of the cabs was in front of the woman's house when the call came through. So, within less than one minute after the woman had called, the cab driver was ringing her door bell.

"Isn't this fast service?" he asked with a big grin on his face.

With a look of surprise she said, "I wouldn't dare ride with anybody who drives as fast as you do." Then she slammed the door in his face.

724. A sympathetic taxi driver had helped the lady and her wheel chair into his cab. As he weaved his way in and out of traffic, he tried to show his concern for her.

"You must find it very difficult to get around in your wheel chair. But, I suppose each of us has some physical problem. Take me for instance. Even with these thick lenses I'm wearing, I can hardly see 50 feet in front of me."

725. A taxi was caught in rush hour traffic and was hardly moving. "Can't you go faster than this?" the passenger asked.

"Yes," the driver said, "but I'm not allowed to leave my cab."

208.

TAXPAYER

726. Two men were chatting about the energy crisis. "Which of our natural resources do you think will become exhausted first?" the first man asked his friend.

"The taxpayer," the other man said.

TEACHER

727. A mother said to her friend, "I don't suppose I ever really appreciated little Jimmy's teacher until last weekend when it rained for two solid days."

728. A school teacher wrote a note home to Jimmy's mother, "Dear Mrs. Jones. Your son, Jimmy, is a smart little boy but he spends all of his time with the girls. I am trying to break him of the habit."

Jimmy's mother wrote back, "I wish you success. Please let me know how you do it. I have been trying for years to break his father of the same habit."

729. A young lady came before the judge of the traffic court to answer the charge of running through a red light. She explained to the judge that she was a school teacher and asked that he take care of her case quickly so that she could get back to her class.

"Well, well," the judge said. "So, you are a school teacher? I have been waiting for years to get a school teacher in my court. You sit right down at that table and write, 'I will not run a red light again,' 500 times."

730. The kindergarten teacher was trying to teach her pupils about money. It was obvious that they all knew what nickels and dimes were, so she took a half dollar out of her purse and tossed it onto the top of her desk. "What's that?" she asked.

A quick reply came from the back of the room: "Tails."

731. The first grade teacher was talking to her class about nature and as she called it "The World Around You."

She asked little Helen in the first row, "Now, Helen, tell everyone in the class. Are you vegetable, animal or mineral."

"I'm not any of those," she replied promptly. "I'm a real live girl."

732. The teacher was trying to impress the class with the importance of doing their school work properly. "Always remember," she said, "work well done never has to be done over again."

"What about when I mow the lawn?" the smart student asked.

733. The first grader had trouble pronouncing any word beginning with the letter R. He called a rabbit a "wabbit" and raspberry jam "waspberry" jam. In order to help him, his teacher gave him this sentence to study: "Robert gave Richard a rap in the ribs for roasting the rabbit so rare."

"Say that over and over and over," she told him, "and we'll see how well you can do when you come back next Monday."

On Monday she called on him to repeat what she had told him, and this is what he said, "Bob gave Dick a poke in the side for not cooking the bunny long enough."

734. It was little Jeannine's first day at school. The teacher was busy getting acquainted with her new students and arranging for seating them properly. "Here," she said to Jeannine, "you may sit in this front row seat for the present."

When little Jeannine was telling her mother about it that evening, she said, "And I sat there all day and the teacher never did give me the present."

735. The student read in a flat monotone, "Where are you going?"

Trying to teach them the elements of expression, the teacher said, "No! Not like that. That's a question. Read it as though you are asking a question. Read it again and notice that little thing at the end of the sentence."

Dutifully, the student read the sentence over. This time he said, "Where are you going, little fishhook looking thing?"

736. A teacher was explaining the importance of penmanship to her first graders. "Remember," she said, "if you don't learn to sign your name, you'll have to pay cash for everything when you grow up."

42, 129, 171, 284, 364, 435, 517, 525, 667, 780.

TEENAGER

737. The youngster was celebrating his 16th birthday.

"Today is the day I promised to let you have your set of car keys," his father said. "You have passed your driving test and have had your learner's permit for three months. Now you can drive the family car."

"Gee, Dad, thanks," the young man said. "And Mom said that if it was all right with you I could take the car tonight on a date. I'm going to pick up my girl and a couple of friends and we're going out on the town. We're going where all the young girls gather and dance and we're going to an outdoor movie where they have an 'X' rated film. This is a sort of celebration for reaching 16 and I sure hope you'll say yes and not try to hold me back."

"Hold you back?" his father said. "I want you to take me with you."

738. Said the man whose 16 year old daughter eloped with her 19 year old boyfriend, "Some of my friends think I've lost a daughter. But really I have gained another teenage driver."

34, 44, 233, 294, 476, 490, 497, 646, 741, 785.

TELEPHONE

739. The caller had given the long distance telephone operator the name of his party, his phone number and the name of the distant city.

"Do you have the area code?" she asked.

"No," he said, "it's just a bug the doctor said is going around."

740. The mother was teaching her six year old to use the telephone. With much careful instruction he dialed his grandmother's number. After about 10 rings it was evident that no one was going to answer. So, mother said, "Go ahead and hang up. I guess nobody's at home."

Eager to make his first telephone call a success, the little boy said, "Not yet. Not yet. I think I hear somebody coming."

741. The father of a teenage daughter was concerned with the amount of time she spent on the telephone; not so much for the time she wasted (he had given up on that long ago), but because nobody else could use the phone. So, as a happy solution, he had a telephone installed for her with her own private number and directory listing.

Two or three days after her telephone had been installed, he came home to find her stretched out on the floor with her feet on the living room couch and chatting away on the family telephone. Her own telephone was resting silently on her dresser. "Why are you using our telephone," he yelled. "Why aren't you talking on your own telephone?"

"I can't," she said, "because I'm expecting an important incoming call on my phone."

742. The girl's mother was faced with a minor emergency and wanted to reach her daughter, who was attending an afternoon ceramics class with a friend. The woman didn't know where the class was being held, and she only knew the last name of her daughter's friend—Wilson. She figured the girl's mother would know where the class was being held and decided to call her.

Being resourceful, she looked up the name Wilson in the phone book and found that there were 12 of them who lived in their side of town. Undaunted, she began with the first one. After about 10 rings, a voice said, "Hello."

"Excuse me," the woman said. "Is this the Wilson home that has a teenage girl who is attending a ceramics class?"

"No," the voice said, "this is the Wilson home where the woman was taking a shower."

162, 163, 380, 401, 537, 707, 810.

TELEVISION

743. A banker who was a boxing fan was going to miss the big fight on television because of an evening board meeting. He called his wife and asked her to please watch the fight on television instead of her regular show.

"I know you have never watched a boxing match," he said, "but you'll understand enough so that you can tell me about it when I get home."

She watched the match, and when her husband came home he rushed into the house and said, "Well, honey, who won the big fight?"

"Nobody," she said. "One of the boxers got hurt in the first round; so they all quit and went home."

744. The television salesman had given a thorough demonstration of the color television set. As a final clincher, he showed how powerful his remote control device was. He showed how it would work in the farthest corner of the house, which happened to be the bathroom connected to the master bedroom.

A few days later, a neighbor asked the housewife how she liked her new television set.

"The picture is beautiful," the woman said, "but it sure is a nuisance to have to go all the way to the bathroom to change channels."

745. Two young ladies were chatting about love, romance and marriage. "The man I marry," the first one said, "must be bright and colorful and entertaining. Yet, when I'm in the mood for peace and quiet, I'll want him to remain silent. I will want him to be up to the minute on sports and politics and the news of the day. And I will want him to stay home nights with me."

Her friend thought for a minute and said, "You don't want a husband; you want a color television set."

746. A newspaper reporter was writing a feature story about prison life and was interviewing one of the prisoners. "Do you watch much television here?"

"Only the daytime shows," the inmate said. "At night we're locked in our cells and don't see any television."

"That's too bad," the reporter said. "But I do think it is nice that the warden lets you watch it in the daytime."

"What do you mean, nice?" the inmate said. "That's part of the punishment."

29, 76, 85, 188, 287, 316, 317, 319, 321, 322, 520, 528.

TEST

747. A man was chatting with his wife at dinner. "We tried something new today at the office. Because we have been hiring a lot of new people in our expansion program, we have decided to give all job applicants an aptitude test. And just to discover what it would show, we had everybody take it, even our oldest employees."

"Did you take it too?" his wife asked.

"Yes," he said, "just for the fun of it."

"What did it show?" she asked.

"Well," he said, "if I didn't own the company, the highest job I could qualify for is janitor."

748. One night in a rainstorm, a man knocked on the door of a man who was running for sheriff. "Can you help me, please," the first man said. "My car has stalled. I think my battery went dead."

"No problem," the candidate said. "I'll get my car and bring my jumping cables, and we'll get it started in no time at all."

When they arrived at the stalled car, the driver surprised the candidate for sheriff by getting into his car and starting it with no trouble. Then he said, "Thanks so much for going to so much trouble to help me. I just wanted to find out what sort of a man you really are. Now, that I know, I'm going to vote for you—and I'm going to tell all my friends about tonight and urge them to vote for you, too."

245.

TESTIMONIAL

749. A widow who had recently married a widower was chatting with a friend.

"How is your new marriage working out?" the friend asked. "I don't want to pry into your affairs, but I understand that one problem with marrying a widower is that he always wants to talk about his first wife. Have you had that trouble?"

"Yes, I did," the woman said. "But I cured him of that."

"You did?" her friend said, "How in the world did you manage that?"

"Whenever he started talking about his first wife," the woman said, "I started talking about my next husband."

TESTIMONY

750. A man was filling in an application for credit. Among the many questions was this: "Length of residence in present location?"

After some mental calculation, he filled in the blank, "Forty to forty-five feet, including the garage."

609, 616, 643, 685.

TEXAS

751. A Texan in his ten-gallon hat and oversized limousine stopped for gasoline in a tiny village in the Tennessee mountains. While the attendant was servicing his car, he struck up a conversation with an old fellow sitting on an overturned nail keg.

"You live around here?" the Texan asked.

"Yep," the man said. "That's my farm just across the road."

"How many acres you got?" the Texan asked.

"Eighty acres, more or less," the man said.

"Only 80 acres?" the Texan said. "Let me tell you about my farm. Why, I get in my car at six o'clock in the morning and I start driving in a straight line and by noon I haven't reached the other side of my farm."

"I know what you mean," the man said. "I've got a car exactly like that myself."

752. A Texan was showing an out-of-state visitor his ranch. As they bumped over a rough dusty road, a bird dashed across in front of the jeep. "That's a bird of paradise," the Texan said.

"He's a long way from home, isn't he?" the visitor answered.

515.

THEATER

753. The opening night of the play had been a disaster. The show was a turkey—no question about it. The story was poor; it was badly written, and the acting was even worse.

Yet, as the curtain came down on the final scene, one man stood up and cheered for the star. "Bravo, bravo, bravo!" he shouted.

Afterwards, a friend said to him, "Why in the world did you cheer that fellow's poor acting? He was terrible."

"Oh," said the first man, "I wasn't cheering for his acting. When I cried 'bravo, bravo,' I was cheering for his plain, unadulterated guts."

TIME

754. The cashier in the restaurant became tired of people asking her what time it was. So, she bought a small electric clock and placed it by her cash register. Now, when people pay their bills they ask her, "Is that clock right?"

512.

TIME PAYMENTS

755. A young lady had graduated from college, been given a well paying job for a large corporation in the city and had settled in her new apartment. Her next move was to buy her first automobile. Her final transaction was with the banker who was arranging the loan for her. When all the papers were in order, she said, "You have been so helpful. How can I ever thank you?"

"Monthly," the banker said. "Monthly."

TIMIDITY

756. The president of Siwash College received this letter: "Dear Mr. President: I am writing about my son, Percy, who is entering college this year as a freshman. Would you please give him special attention and sort of keep an eye on him. Percy is a rather sensitive young man. Although he is 22 years old, he has lived a rather sheltered life. He is extremely shy and not used to mixing with people. I hope you will help him get adjusted. You'll understand my concern when I tell you that this is the first time Percy has ever been away from home—except for three years in the U.S. Navy."

TOURIST

757. A tourist came to a country village where the main road came to a dead end. Directly in front of him was a sign which said, "Arlington, 6 miles." Beneath the sign were two arrows, one pointing to the right, the other to the left.

The tourist stopped his car and said to a man leaning against the telephone pole, "Does it matter which road I take to Arlington?"

"Not to me it doesn't," said the helpful native.

758. Two women were taking the sightseeing tour of Mount Vernon, the beautiful home of George Washington. After they had walked through the house and grounds and were returning to town on the bus, one woman said to the other, "Wasn't it impressive?"

"It certainly was," her friend said. "And did you notice that the entire house was furnished in Early American?"

759. A man and his wife were traveling out West and stopped in an Indian trading post in New Mexico. As they were browsing through the store they noticed an Indian woman standing near a large display of moccasins. The clerk walked up to her and said, "Squaw needum moccasins?"

She turned to him and said in a clear voice with no trace of accent, "No, thank you, I'm just waiting for my husband." And then with a twinkle in her eye she said, "You needum learn English?"

760. Two old-timers were sitting and chatting on the front steps of a country store when a car with two strangers pulled up. "Hey," shouted one of the men. "How long has this wide place in the road been dead?"

"I don't know," one of the old-timers said. "You are the first two buzzards we've seen."

761. A tourist stopped at a fancy resort motel and went in to register.

"What are your rates?" he asked.

"A room on the first floor," said the clerk, "is $50, on the second floor $40, and on the third floor $30."

As the man shook his head and turned to leave, the clerk said, "Aren't you going to register? Don't you find our motel attractive enough?"

"Oh," said the man, "it's attractive enough, but it just isn't tall enough."

762. The bus load of tourists had stopped at an Indian trading post near Albuquerque. One woman bought several items including a peace pipe. As she was paying for her purchases she noticed some finely printed characters on the pipe stem.

"I am sure this is Indian language," she said to the Indian cashier. "I wonder if you can translate it for me."

"I'd be glad to," the Indian said. "It says 'The Attorney General has determined that smoking is hazardous to your health.' "

763. Two natives who lived on the outskirts of a tourist resort out West were chatting.

"They tell me there was a bit of excitement in town yesterday," one of them said. "A man had a heart attack and dropped dead in front of the Indian trading post."

"Yes, there was a lot of excitement for a few minutes," his friend said. "Then they discovered it wasn't as bad as they thought it was. Turned out to be a tourist."

406, 551, 692.

TRAFFIC

764. Because of an accident on the Interstate highway near a large city during the morning rush hour, traffic had backed up for several miles and was at a standstill. After sitting in his car without moving for half an hour, one irate motorist walked half a mile to a telephone and called the city police department to protest.

"I'm sorry," the desk sergeant said, "but that portion of the highway is in the county and out of our jurisdiction."

The man then called the Sheriff's department and was told, "That portion of the road is in the county all right, but it is Interstate and is under the jurisdiction of the State Highway Patrol."

The man then called the State Highway Patrol and began to complain. He was interrupted by the receptionist who said, "I'm sorry, there isn't anyone here right now who can help you. They haven't been able to get to work this morning on account of a huge traffic jam on the Interstate."

765. The patrolman had pulled the car over to the side of the road and was preparing to give the driver a citation when he was distracted by the woman sitting next to the driver.

"See?" she screamed. "What did I tell you? I told you not to drive so fast. And besides, you always drive in the wrong lane and you don't turn on your signals. Besides that you weave back and forth from lane to lane. I told you you'd get arrested someday. What have you got to say, now?"

The patrolman said to the driver, "Who is that woman?"

"That's my wife," the driver said.

"Well, drive on," the patrolman said. "You've got enough trouble without me giving you a traffic ticket."

766. A highway patrolman had stopped a car for speeding and was writing a traffic violation ticket for the driver.

"You don't know who I am," the driver said, "I'm Chairman of the Board of County Commissioners. I'm late for a Board meeting at the Court House. You should let me continue because the meeting can't start until I get there."

"I understand your problem," the patrolman said, "and I'm writing this ticket just as fast as I can."

767. Experienced travelers have learned not to arrive in a city during the rush hour, even on the Interstate highways. Now and then, however, the smartest drivers get caught in bumper to bumper situations. So it was with a woman who found herself at 7:30 one evening in a three-mile-long line of cars inching their way across the Mississippi River bridge at New Orleans. As she sat in her car waiting for traffic to move, she shouted to a driver in the next lane, "This is terrible. I'm sure thankful I didn't get caught in the 5:30 traffic."

The driver of the other car shouted back and said, "I hate to upset you, lady, but this *is* the 5:30 traffic."

768. A man had just been fined $35.00 for a moving traffic violation. When he paid his fine he was given a receipt by the clerk of court.

Unhappy about the fine, the man grumbled, "What good is this receipt?"

"You should file it in a handy place," the clerk said, "because when you have five of them, you get a bicycle."

418, 428, 484, 725.

TRANQUILIZERS

769. The doctor had prescribed tranquilizers for his patient who asked him, "Are these pills habit forming?"

"No," the doctor said, "not as long as you take them regularly."

770. The personnel director of a large company was in constant turmoil over employee problems. One evening while he was reading a newspaper article about how tension and stress drive some people to drugs, he said to his wife, "I can understand that. I'd probably be on drugs myself if I weren't taking tranquilizers."

556, 611.

TRANSLATION

771. The scene was a cocktail party at the Brazilian Embassy in Washington. As the crowd increased in size, there was much hugging and hand shaking in the South American style and much chit-chat in a dozen different languages. One young man from the U.S. State Department joined a circle of women who were talking English—mostly with a strong accent. But one woman, dressed in typical South American attire, was speaking perfect English. Wishing to say something complimentary to the lady he said, "You certainly do speak English well—and with no trace of an accent, either."

"Well, I should," she said. "I'm the wife of the congressman from the 19th District of Tennessee, and I was born in Indiana."

762.

TRAVEL

772. A man and his wife had arrived at the airport by taxi and were carrying their bags toward the check-in counter when he said, "I think we packed everything we need for our vacation, but I sure do wish we had brought the kitchen table."

"What?" his wife said. "That's a silly thing to say. Why do you wish we had brought the kitchen table?"

"Because I left our tickets on it."

773. A man in a high powered car swung off the highway onto a gravel patch in front of a typical back country store. Several old-timers were sitting on the porch chatting and chewing tobacco. As the driver braked the car to a fast stop, he yelled at the men on the porch, "I want to go to Farmingdale."

After 10 or 15 seconds when no one had responded, he shouted again, "I want to go to Farmingdale."

The men on the porch seemed to be holding a whispering consultation for a moment, and then one of the old fellows walked over to the car and said, "Mister, we just had a committee meeting and we have no objection."

774. An American and his wife were traveling through Spain and found themselves in an out-of-the way village at lunch time. Whereas in Madrid and the larger cities they had no language problem, they discovered that in this small town, nobody spoke English.

"Well," said her husband, "that really isn't much of a problem if we will use a little common sense. Here is a place that is obviously a restaurant. Let's go in."

He was right. It was a restaurant. As soon as the couple were seated a waiter came with a menu. "Do you speak English?" the American asked.

The waiter did not say anything but pointed to the menu.

The man's wife said, "Now, what? You can't read the menu and he can't understand anything you say. Let's see your common sense get you out of this hole."

"No problem," her husband said. "Watch me order two steaks smothered with mushrooms." He took the menu, turned to the back, which was blank, and put down the figure 2 and after it he drew a rough sketch of a cow then added a huge mushroom. After he had finished his writing and drawing, he handed it to the waiter.

The waiter smiled from ear to ear, nodded his head and said, "Si, senor."

Two minutes later he returned with two tickets to a bull fight and an umbrella.

775. A woman was telling a friend about plans for her vacation: "I'm going out West. I'm planning to visit Yellowstone National Park."

"If you go to Yellowstone," her friend said, "don't forget Old Faithful."

"Oh, I'm not," the woman said. "He's going with me."

776. Two women were chatting at the club house. "I was talking with Jean the other day about vacation plans and she tells me that you aren't going to Paris this summer."

"No," her friend replied, "that was last year. This year we aren't going to Rome."

28, 250, 344, 645, 692, 763, 799.

TRUST

777. A man asked a friend to lend him 20 dollars. Without any hesitation the friend reached in his wallet and took out a 10 dollar bill and handed it to the man.

"Thanks," the man said, "but I asked for 20 dollars and this is only 10."

"That's right," the friend said. "This way we break even. You lose 10. I lose 10."

778. When a man tells you he is the boss at his home, don't believe anything he says. Because a fellow who will lie about that will lie about anything.

TRUTH

779. The man who was called on to address 1,200 men and women at the Chamber of Commerce banquet was rushed to the hospital the day before the big event. As the surgeon cut open his stomach, a flock of butterflies flew out. "Well, I'll be darned," the surgeon said. "He *was* telling the truth."

780. "Today," the teacher said to her first graders, "we are celebrating George Washington's birthday. He was a great man and had overcome many, many problems. Can anyone tell me one problem that he had?"

"Yes," said a little boy in the front row. "He couldn't tell a lie."

781. Two college roommates were chatting about boys. "If a fellow took you to a football game," the first girl asked, "and after that to dinner, and the next night he took you to a dance, and the next night to a drive-in movie, and the next night to a nightclub and he never did try to kiss you, what would you do?"

Her friend gave her a quick reply. "I'd lie about it."

782. A woman and her husband were invited to her rich aunt's home for dinner. "Be sure to be nice to my aunt," the wife said, "because she is getting up in years and likes attention."

After dinner had been served and the dessert came, her aunt explained that she had baked the cake herself, from an original recipe. The niece's husband ate a huge piece of it and said, "I must say this is the best cake I have ever tasted."

On the way home from the party, his wife said, "Why did you say that was the best cake you had ever tasted? It was awful. I bake better cakes than that all the time."

"I know you do," her husband said. "You told me to be nice to her and I told the truth when I said, *I must say* this is the best cake I ever tasted."

14, 22, 100, 225, 277, 660, 708.

UNDERSTANDING

783. A mother heard her four year old son screaming and rushed into the recreation room to see what was happening. There he sat while his baby sister was pulling his hair with all her might.

"Don't let it bother you," the mother said. "Your little sister doesn't know that it hurts you."

A few minutes after she had left the room she heard more screaming. This time, when she rushed into the room she found the baby crying.

"What's the matter with the baby?" she asked the four-year-old.

"Nothing much," he said, "except now she knows."

784. "My, what pretty roses," the lady said as the man stopped his flower cart in front of her house. "I don't want any today, but if you will come by next Thursday morning, I would like to buy six or seven dozen to decorate the living room. My daughter is coming out that day, and I want everything to look as lovely as I can."

"Thanks, lady," the man said. "I'll be here. And I'll bring the prettiest roses I can find. I know how you feel about your daughter coming out. What was she in for?"

785. A man was applying for his driver's license. The young lady at the application desk was a bit officious and uppity as she explained to him, "Look, it's people like you who cause all of the delay here. You must fill in every blank on the form and check every little box. Besides, when we ask for your middle name, we don't want your middle initial. And besides, it looks like you have put your first name first when it should be last. If you'll go over to that desk and fill it out properly, I can take care of it for you."

The man never said a word. Instead he did exactly as he was told and returned in a few minutes. In the meantime, the young lady realized she had been a bit harsh with him and she said, "I'm sorry I seemed rude a few minutes ago, but this has been on of those days, if you know what I mean."

"Yes," he said, "I know what you mean. And please don't let it worry you. I'm used to being pushed around a bit. I have three teenagers."

786. A man and his wife and their nine children drove to Florida for a week's stay at Disneyworld. They had been gone about four days when they sent a post card to their next door neighbor. "We are enjoying every minute of our vacation. We hope you are, too."

5, 155, 358, 564, 800.

UNEMPLOYED

787. The boss was firing one of his assistant bookkeepers. "I am sorry we have to let you go," he said, "but it should make you proud to know we are paying $350,000 for the computer that is replacing you."

788. A man in the bookkeeping department was being laid off. His boss wanted to break the news as gently as he could; so he said, "I'm sorry, Joe, but because we are automating our department, we are reducing our accounting personnel by half."

"Do you mean I'm being replaced by a computer?" the man asked.

"Not exactly," his boss said. "In your case it isn't an entire computer—just a transistor."

260, 278.

USED CAR

789. "How's that used car you bought last week?" a man asked his friend.

"Terrible," his friend said. "You never heard so may rattles. Everything on it makes a noise except the horn."

790. A man and his wife were shopping for a used car. They were highly impressed with a shiny sports model that the salesman seemed overly anxious to sell. "This car was owned by a little old lady wearing tennis shoes," she said. "She drove it only five times. You will note that it has just a thousand miles on it. You'll find it is a great bargain."

Being a bit cautious, they checked the name on the registration certificate and called the woman and told her what the salesman had said.

"That's right. He told the truth," she said. "I'm sixty-two years old and I always wear tennis shoes when I drive. The thousand miles on the odometer is correct. I've only run it in five 200-mile stock car races. I came in second twice, third place twice and would have finished in the money in the last race except that I blew an engine."

791. "I see you finally traded in that old beat up car of yours," a man said to his friend.

"Yes," the man said. "I finally got tired of explaining it to the police; so I got rid of it."

"What do you mean when you say explaining it to the police?" the first man asked.

"Every time I parked it," the first man said, "the police would ask me if I had reported the accident."

658.

VACATION

792. A woman read in the paper that some businesses were putting notes on their safes which read, "Notice, no money kept in this safe, only company documents." The idea was that burglars wouldn't tear up a safe and destroy papers looking for money and other valuables.

So, when she would leave her house she would put this note on the box that held her jewelry: "The jewelry in this box is imitation. All of my genuine pieces are in the safe deposit box at the bank."

One time, she came home after a party and found her jewelry stolen, and this note was in its place. "I took it anyway because I myself am a substitute. The regular burglar who works this territory is in Florida on his vacation."

793. "Where did you and your husband go on your vacation this year?" a woman asked her friend.

"We had a marvelous time in Curacao," her friend said.

"I've never heard of Curacao," the first woman said. "Where is that?"

"I don't know," her friend said. "We flew."

794. A resort hotel in Naples, Florida carried this bit of puffery in its brochure. "Our hotel is noted for its peace and quiet. We are located off the beaten path—away from the maddening crowd. If it's solitude you are looking for, you will find it here. (Please make your reservations early because our 600 luxurious rooms are always sold out months ahead of the season with hundreds on the waiting list.)"

795. A farmer and his wife were visiting Washington, D.C. This was the first time they had ever been away from the farm—the first time they had ever stayed in a hotel. As they were checking in, the farmer asked the desk clerk about a place to eat.

"We serve your meals right here in the hotel," he said. "Breakfast from 6:30 to 11:30; lunch from 12:00 until 2:30; dinner from 5:30 until midnight."

"My goodness," the farmer's wife whispered to him, "when will we have time to do any sightseeing?"

796. A farmer was chatting with a friend in front of the post office. "My wife and I are repairin' to take a trip up North."

His friend said, "I don't like to correct you, but you mean that you are preparing to go on a trip up North—not repairing. To repair means to fix."

"That's right," the farmer said. "My wife and I are fixin' to take a trip up North."

797. A salesman who covered the Southeast for a large company in Chicago called the home office from Miami. "I'm stuck here," he said. "We're in the middle of a hurricane. The airlines have stopped flying. The busses and trains have stopped. The highways are flooded. What do you think I should do?"

Without a moment's hesitation, the sales manager said, "Start your two-week summer vacation as of this morning."

798. A man was chatting with his friend about their summer vacation plans. "This summer I plan to take a Caribbean cruise," the first man said. "Last year I took a honeydew vacation and I had all I want of that."

"What in the world is a honeydew vacation?" his friend asked.

"Oh," the first man said, "that's when you stay home and your wife keeps saying, 'honey do this,' and 'honey do that.' "

799. Two friends were chatting about their vacations. "We went to Europe this year," the first woman said. "We visited France, Spain, Italy and Switzerland."

"Did you go to Venice?" her friend asked.

"We had planned to stay a week there," the first woman said, "but they had been having a lot of rain lately, and we arrived to find all the streets flooded. Everyone was going up and down in boats, so we didn't even stay overnight. We went on to Rome."

800. A man and his wife, both with senior citizen status, were vacationing in Ft. Lauderdale. While the wife spent most of her time at the country club playing bridge, her husband played shuffleboard, walked up and down the beach and otherwise spent his time outdoors.

One afternoon a gossipy acquaintance sought out the wife and whispered in her ear, "Guess what? I was over on the beach about an hour ago and saw you husband strolling up the beach with a cute little blond on his arm—and she was wearing a bikini, too."

"Well," said the understanding and tolerant wife, "what did you expect him to have on his arm at his age, a toy shovel and pail?"

27, 504, 775, 776, 786.

VALENTINE'S DAY

801. A young man was trying to impress his new girlfriend with a lot of sentimental and romantic conversation. "Just think," he said, "tomorrow is Valentine's Day. That is the day for lovers. That is the day when two hearts become as one. And to think that last year at this time, I hadn't even met you, my darling."

"Isn't it wonderful?" his girlfriend said as she snuggled up in his arms. "But, let's not talk about your past. Let's talk about my present."

VANITY

802. At a luncheon meeting, a man almost failed to speak to an old friend because he didn't recognize him. "Hey, Harry," he said, "I almost passed you by. I didn't recognize you with the glasses. When did you start wearing them?"

"Last week," his friend said. "I have been needing them for a long time, but it was only last week that my curiosity became greater than my vanity."

VETERINARIAN

803. A veterinarian decided to run for Congress. The campaign was hot and furious and nasty. The night before the election, the candidates appeared on a television debate. During one heated exchange, the veterinarian's opponent said, "Everywhere you go, people call you doctor. Isn't that just a come-on. Are you really a veterinarian?"

"Why do you ask?" the veterinarian said. "Have you suddenly become sick?"

VOTE

804. Two friends were chatting about the candidates for Congress. "I don't like either one of them," the first man said. "I think we're lucky that only one of them is going to Washington."

572, 607.

WAITER

805. The young doctor had worked his way through medical school by waiting on tables in a restaurant. As most students are, he was very nervous when he examined his first patient. In giving her his report, he said, "Heart okay, liver fine, kidneys excellent—and you have a choice of two vegetables, a salad, coffee, tea or milk and a dessert from the cart."

WAITING

806. As the line of people was waiting for the bus, several of them were following the progress of the astronauts on their portable radios. "Hey," said one of the men in line, "think of the wonders of modern science. The astronauts already have circled the earth one time while we have been standing here waiting for the bus."

547.

WALKING

807. A man was walking down a country road and called to a farmer working in his field, "How far is it to the nearest filling station?"

"About six miles," the farmer said, "as the the crow flies."

"How far is it," the man said, "if the crow has to walk and carry an empty gasoline can?"

WASHINGTON

808. A man who had left home to go to Washington to work was visiting his home town and was chatting with an old friend

"You've got it made," his friend said. "I read about all you bureaucrats and all of your fringe benefits. What do they mean by that? Do you have any?"

Yes," said the bureaucrat, "I have a few. Like for instance, health care, and half-price meals at the department cafeteria, a good pension plan, tenure in my job, and my own parking place."

"Is that all of them?" his friend asked.

"No, there's one more," the bureaucrat said. "That's spending somebody else's money."

809. A man and his wife were visiting Washington, D.C. for the first time with their two children. They had signed up for a tour of the city, and as they were riding up Pennsylvania Avenue the tour guide said, "On your right is the National Archives Building. You will notice the inscription over the entrance which says, 'The Past is Prologue.' "

"What does that mean?" one of the children asked her father.

"Liberally translated," he said, "that means, 'you ain't seen nothing yet.' "

810. One day the phone rang at Republican National Headquarters and a worried voice asked, "Can you please tell me the name of the Democratic Candidate for Governor of Virginia?"

The person at Republican Headquarters thought for a moment and then said, "I'm sorry, I don't know. But, why don't you call the Democratic National Committee. I'm sure they can tell you."

And then a sad voice replied, "This is the Democratic National Committee."

WEATHER

811. A woman was talking to her husband at dinner. "I went to see the doctor today," she said, "and he told me I am in bad shape and that I need a complete change of climate. I'd like to spend a week in the mountains."

"No need to go to the mountains," her husband said. "Just stick around here next week. The weather man on TV said we are going to have a complete change in the climate. A hurricane is on the way."

812. As two friends were preparing to push off from the dock in their fishing boat, a sudden rain squall came up. The water came down in torrents. "Do you think it will stop?" asked the first fellow.

"It always has," said his friend.

813. A man and his wife were caught in a sudden rain storm one evening as they emerged from the theater and were passing in front of a fancy night club.

"We have a choice," the man said to his wife. "We can either stand out here and get wet or go inside and get soaked."

617, 668.

WIDOW

814. The debating team had lost in the state finals, and the entire speech class was dejected and down in the dumps.

Trying to cheer them up, the teacher said, "You can't be first all the time. Even great men have to be second once in awhile."

"What about George Washington?" a smart student demanded. "He was the first President, first in war, first in peace and first in the hearts of his countrymen."

"That's right," said the teacher. "But, remember, he married a widow."

413, 674.

WIFE

815. A woman who felt a little neglected because her husband never noticed what she was wearing decided she would get his attention once and for all.

One evening they were invited for dinner at a friend's house. As they were getting in their car to drive out of the garage, the man looked at his wife. "What in the world are you wearing?" he shouted. "That's nothing but your see-through nightgown."

She smiled at him and said, "Now that you have noticed what I'm wearing for a change, I'll rush back into the house and slip on a dress."

816. "You have been charged with vagrancy," the judge said to the prisoner before him. "And I'm going to sentence you to 60 days in the workhouse because you have no visible means of support."

"Oh, yes I have, judge," the man said. "I've got a wife. Honey, come stand up here where the judge can see you."

817. A woman said to her friend, "My, you look tired. You must have had a trying day."

"I certainly did," the first woman said. "I chased all over town all morning trying to get something for my husband."

"Did you have many offers?" her friend asked.

39, 40, 170, 304, 381, 403, 719, 749.

WOMEN

818. "Did I understand you rightly when you said that you never fool around with women?"

"That's right. When it comes to women, I don't fool around."

WOMEN'S LIB

819. "What do you think of the women's lib movement?" one young lady asked her friend.

"I think I would like to be liberated," she said, "but first I want to be captured."

820. Two young ladies were chatting at lunch. "I have just joined the women's lib movement," the first one said.

"What kind of liberation are you looking for?" her friend asked.

"I want to get married," the first one said, "and not have to work anymore."

WORDS

821. Here are some four-letter words that will shock any bride: cook, wash, dust, iron.

WORK

822. The young man had just been hired as a buyer for a large department store.

"I hope you will enjoy working here," the personnel director said.

"I'm sure I will," the young man said. "I have always thought this was one of the greatest department stores in the country, and I'll do my best to be worthy of your confidence in hiring me."

"I am sure you will," the personnel man said. "And you'll succeed if you just keep in mind our slogan for the Buying Department."

"What is the slogan?" the young man asked.

"Buy good—or goodbye," the personnel director said.

823. The owner of a lumber yard arrived at 7:00 A.M. to open business and found that his assistant manager was already on the job. "What are you doing here so early?" he asked. "You don't have to come to work until eight o'clock."

"Well," the assistant manager said, "it's like this. I didn't get home until three o'clock this morning. As I was undressing, my wife woke up and said, 'Aren't you getting up mighty early this morning?' So, to keep from having an argument, I put on my clothes again and came to work."

824. A tourist had stopped by the roadside to have his picnic lunch and to relax and look over the countryside. He struck up a conversation with a farmer who was working near the fence.

"You have a beautiful farm here," the tourist said. "What do you raise?"

"Oh," the farmer said, "a bit of this and that. Corn, beans, some carrots, cabbage, okra."

"It must keep you busy," the tourist said. "What time do you go to work every day?"

"I don't go to work," the farmer said. "I live right in the middle of it."

146, 165, 259, 260, 270, 271, 278, 409, 419, 442, 519, 718, 820.

WRITER

825. A businessman was stopped by a panhandler who asked him for a dollar. The businessman said, "Why don't you find a job instead of begging? There are plenty of jobs if you will only look for one."

"Oh, I have a profession. I really am an author. I wrote a best-seller once titled, *Five Hundred Money Making Ideas.*"

"Then, why are you begging?" the business man wanted to know.

"This," said the panhandler, "is one of the ways."

826. The would-be author had written his first novel and put it in the mail to a large publishing house. On the first page, he wrote this disclaimer. "All characters in this book are products of my own imagination. Any resemblance to any person, living or dead, is purely coincidental."

When he received his manuscript back with a rejection slip, he found that first page statement circled in red with this comment: "That's what's wrong with it."

WRITING

827. An elderly little woman spoke to a man who was buying stamps at the post office. "Would you please do me a favor?" she asked. "Do you mind addressing this envelope for me?"

He was happy to help the little woman, and he did as she asked. Then she asked him to write a short message on a sheet of paper that she gave him. He did that, too, and then said, "Is there anything else I can do for you?"

"Yes, if you don't mind," she said. "Will you please write at the bottom of my letter, 'please excuse this poor handwriting.' "

160, 736.

YOUTH

828. There isn't much wrong with the younger generation that getting married, becoming a parent, buying a house on time and becoming a taxpayer won't cure.

ZOO

829. A first grade school teacher was taking her pupils on a field trip to the local zoo. Each child was given a turn at guessing the names of the various animals. The camel, lion, giraffe, bear, and the elephant all were named correctly.

"Now, it's your turn," the teacher said to a little girl. She pointed to a deer and said, "What is the name of that animal?"

The little girl hesitated for a long time, and the teacher tried to prompt her by saying, "Think hard. What does you mother call your father at home?"

"So *that's* what a baboon looks like!" the little girl exclaimed.

516.

THEMATIC INDEX

ANOTHER WAY TO FIND A STORY

Look among these 605 subjects to find a story not listed under a main category.

The numbers indicate the number of the story —not the page number.